Shuire Flu.

EXPLORING IRELAND'S CASTLES

EXPLORING IRELAND'S CASTLES

TARQUIN BLAKE

The Collins Press

Oh! bright are the names of the chieftains and sages,
That shine like the stars through the darkness of ages,
Whose deeds are inscribed on the pages of story,
There for ever to live in the sunshine of glory,
Heroes of history, phantoms of fable,
Charlemagne's champions, and Arthur's Round Table;
Oh! but they all a new lustre could borrow
From the glory that hangs round the name of MacCaura! …

… But, oh! proud MacCaura, what anguish to touch on
The fatal stain of thy princely escutcheon;
In thy story's bright garden the one spot of bleakness,
Through ages of valour the one hour of weakness!
Thou, the heir of a thousand chiefs, sceptred and royal –
Thou to kneel to the Norman and swear to be loyal!
Oh! a long night of horror, and outrage, and sorrow,
Have we wept for thy treason, base Diarmid MacCaura!

Oh! why ere you thus to the foreigner pandered,
Did you not bravely call round your emerald standard,
The chiefs of your house of Lough Lene and Clan Awley
O'Donogh, MacPatrick, O'Driscoll, MacAwley,
O'Sullivan More, from the towers of Dunkerron,
And O'Mahon, the chieftain of green Ardinterran?
As the sling sends the stone or the bent bow the arrow,
Every chief would have come at the call of MacCaura.

Soon, soon didst thou pay for that error in woe,
Thy life to the Butler, thy crown to the foe,
Thy castles dismantled, and strewn on the sod,
And the homes of the weak, and the abbeys of God!
No more in thy halls is the wayfarer fed,
Nor the rich mead sent round, nor the soft heather spread,
Nor the 'clairsech's' sweet notes, now in mirth, now in sorrow,
All, all have gone by, but the name of MacCaura!

MacCaura, the pride of thy house is gone by,
But its name cannot fade, and its fame cannot die,
Though the Arigideen, with its silver waves, shine
Around no green forests or castles of thine –
Though the shrines that you founded no incense doth hallow,
Nor hymns float in peace down the echoing Allo,
One treasure thou keepest, one hope for the morrow –
True hearts yet beat of the clan of MacCaura!

'The Clan of MacCaura' by Denis Florence MacCarthy, 1882

First published in 2017 by
The Collins Press
West Link Park
Doughcloyne
Wilton
Cork
T12 N5EF
Ireland

A CIP record for this book is available from the British Library.

Hardback ISBN: 978-1-84889-326-9

Design and typesetting by Anú Design, Tara
Typeset in Garamond
Printed in Spain by LiberDúplex

Photographs
Page ii: Leap Castle, County Offaly: the second-floor 'bloody chapel'; page v: view from basement of south tower,
Kilwaughter Castle, County Antrim; page vii (l–r): Dunguaire Castle, County Galway; main staircase, Charleville Forest
Castle, County Offaly; Lackeen Castle, County Tipperary; Burncourt Castle, County Tipperary, view through south-east
entrance; page viii: Malahide Castle, County Dublin; page ix (l–r): Scrabo Tower, County Down; entrance corridor at Johnstown Castle,
County Wexford; carved stone head at Kilkenny Castle, County Kilkenny; first-floor saloon, Charleville Forest Castle, County Offaly.

Disclaimer: Readers should note that this is an information guide and does not act as an invitation to enter any of the
properties or sites listed. Some of the properties listed are in private hands and permission would be required from the owner
before visiting. Ruins are hazardous. Responsibility cannot be accepted by the author or publisher for any loss, injury or
inconvenience sustained by anyone as a result of using this book.

Contents

Preface

I started working on this book after receiving various requests. The basis was that the book should include the major Irish castles and a combination of both occupied and ruined castles. Other criteria were that the castles must be photogenic, that there must be recorded history (the majority of ruined tower houses do not even have a record of their builder, thus making them very difficult to write about), and also that all the main periods of castle building are represented: the Anglo-Norman and royal fortresses such as Trim and Limerick, tower houses, fortified houses and also neo-Gothic castles. I excluded some castles that I have previously photographed and written about in my earlier books and some of the castles that I initially selected could not be included because I was unable to secure permission to photograph from their owners. I have deliberately included some lesser-known castles such as Fiddaun and Menlo castles, both in County Galway, which are magical places to visit. Finally, this book is not intended to be a history of medieval castles, as this has already been well covered in the excellent books David Sweetman's *The Medieval Castles of Ireland* and Tom McNeill's *Castles in Ireland*.

Acknowledgements

Many thanks to everybody who has helped me with this book. Thanks to: Lord and Lady Rosse for their help on Birr Castle, Bridget Vance and Dudley Stewart for their help at Charleville Forest Castle, Rebecca Armstrong for her help at Clonony Castle, Matt Wheeler for his help at Johnston Castle, Jaki Jordan and the OPW staff at Kilkenny Castle, Anne Blackmore and Linda Hooke for their help at Kilwaughter Castle, Pat Lavelle for his help at Kylemore Castle, Sean Ryan for his help at Leap Castle, Lord Burlington, Helen Hardway, and all the staff at Lismore Castle, Carrie, Susie and Peter for their help at Lough Cutra Castle, Valerie Pakenham for her help at Tullynally Castle. Many thanks to the Department of the Environment, the OPW, and to Shannon Heritage.

A big thank-you to my proof-readers: Alison, Fiona and Margaret Reilly and Marie Conlin.

Rathgall Hill Fort,
County Wicklow

Introduction

The *Oxford English Dictionary* defines a castle as: 'a large building, typically of the medieval period, fortified against attack with thick walls, battlements, towers, and often a moat.'

Although not really meeting this definition of a castle, the earliest Irish defensive structures were the Late Bronze Age/Iron Age hill forts, where walls and ditches follow the contours of a hill, to enclose an area as a defended settlement. A good example, and one of the earliest, can be found at Rathgall in County Wicklow. Here three outer ramparts, built of stone and earth, dating from around 1400 to 1000 BC, enclose an area of about 18 acres. At the centre is a much later inner rampart, or ring fort, enclosing an area about 45 metres in diameter. Ring forts were typically built in the early medieval period, between AD 500 and 900, and are by far the most common archaeological field monument in Ireland. The remains of more than 45,000 ring forts can be found scattered across the country. Comprising earthen or stone-built enclosures, they were the farmsteads of their time, designed to offer basic defence to their inhabitants and their cattle, usually from predators such as wolves. They were not designed for warfare, though may have helped fend off a fleeting attack by raiders. An excellent example can be found at Leacanabuile in County Kerry.

By the end of the eleventh century, the Normans had conquered England and their concept of using martial supremacy to capture new territory, along with their military building methods were beginning to be used in Ireland. In 1129, according to the early Irish manuscript, the *Annals of Loch Cé*, Turlough O'Conor, King of Connacht, erected a *caislean* (castle) at Athlone. His intention was to use this as a base for raids eastwards into Meath. Nothing of this early castle survives and there is no recorded description, though the Annals of Clonmacnoise record that it was 'burned by a thunderbolt' in 1131, implying the castle was built of timber. Other early fortifications were recorded

at Ballinasloe, Galway, Collooney, Cuileanntrach, Tuam and Ferns. All were built, demolished or burnt between the years 1124 and 1166, and have no surviving remnants. There is some debate about the form of these early fortifications. They may have been earthwork ring forts or motte-and-bailey castles, which were built across northern Europe from the tenth century onwards.

The motte-and-bailey castle typically comprised the motte, a flat-topped mound, around 10 metres high and 20 metres in diameter, which was connected by a wooden gangway or bridge to the bailey, a larger courtyard about 30 metres in diameter, built at ground level. Both were surrounded by a palisade of heavy timber, which in turn was surrounded by a deep ditch, the digging of which provided the earth to construct the motte. On the summit of the motte a wooden tower was built, which would house the commander and provide a place of retreat in case of attack, whilst the majority of the troops would be quartered in huts within the bailey.

The Anglo-Norman invasion of Ireland initially began in 1169 with their arrival in Wexford. Richard de Clare (Strongbow) followed in 1170 and King Henry II in 1171. Numerous motte-and-bailey castles were constructed in the following decades and more than 470 can still be identified today. The motte at Granard in County Longford is an excellent example and is thought to be the highest in the country. Here the Anglo-Norman knight Sir Richard de Tuite dug a deep ditch around a natural hillock, depositing the excavated rock and soil on top, to form a steep 10-metre-high mound. On the south side are the remains of a large D-shaped bailey, also surrounded by massive earth banks and a second ditch.

The Anglo-Normans had superior weapons and military tactics, but the Irish were far more numerous and were also fearless and reckless in warfare. The Anglo-Normans soon realised they would need to build more permanent and more defensible fortresses if they were to hold their Irish territory and expand their control.

In 1172, Roderick O'Connor, King of Connacht, attacked Hugh de Lacy's earthwork castle at Trim in County Meath. Within a few years de Lacy began rebuilding the castle in stone, and so followed one of Ireland's first stone castles (see p. 204). At first a strong, stone-built rectangular tower, surrounded by a substantial curtain wall was found to be sufficient to keep the native Irish at bay.

Elsewhere, King Henry had seized the ports of Dublin, Waterford and Wexford but had no real centre of English royal power in Ireland. His son, King John, began building the two main early royal castles, Dublin Castle in 1204, and Limerick Castle (see p. 130) in 1211. The royal castles were usually built without a keep, the plan being based instead on a strong curtain wall with towers, surrounding a roughly rectangular enclosure.

The taking of Ireland by the English was fragmented and with many setbacks so that even after 300 years, the English only had full control of the Pale (parts of the modern counties of Dublin, Louth, Meath, and Kildare), and a few other towns. By the start of the fifteenth century, the English Crown, alarmed at the frequent Irish invasions into the Pale, decided to encourage loyal English residents to build castles by offering them a subsidy towards construction costs. A statute, issued by Henry VI, states 'it is agreed and asserted that every liege man of our Lord, the King of the said Counties [the Pale] who chooses to build a Castle or Tower House sufficiently embattled or fortified, wither the next ten years to wit twenty feet in length, sixteen feet in width and forty feet in height or more, that the commons of the said Counties shall pay to the said person, to build the said Castle or Tower £10 by way of subsidy'.

Comparing the historical cost of a building project, £10 is roughly the equivalent of over €60,000 in today's money. Not surprisingly, what followed was a period of very rapid construction of castles. They often followed Henry's minimum measurements of a rectangular structure measuring about 6 metres by 5 metres and 12 metres high. Henry's offer in fact proved so popular in County Meath that in 1449 a limit was put on the number of castles that could be built in that county. In other parts of Ireland, even without the support of the subsidy, tower houses became the preferred residence of the Irish chieftain and the English gentleman alike. It is estimated more than 7,000 were built, and by the Late Middle Ages, Ireland was by far the most castellated country in the whole of Europe. These fairly modest castles, known as tower houses, are today, by a long way, the most prevalent ruin that can be found in the Irish countryside. An excellent example is Fiddaun Castle in County Galway (see p. 102).

There are very few contemporary accounts of life inside the Irish tower house. Luke Gernon recorded a visit to a tower house in his 1620 manuscript, *A Discourse of Ireland*:

Granard Motte, County Longford

The lady of the house meets you with her trayne. Salutations past. You shall be presented with all the drinks of the house. First the ordinary beere, then sacke [fortified wine], then old ale. The lady tasted it, you must not refuse it. The fyre is prepared in the middle of the hall, where you may solace yourself till supper time. You shall not want for sacke or tobacco. By this time the table is spread and plentifully furnished with a variety of meats, but is cooked without sauce. They feast together with great jollity and healths [toasts] around. Towards the middle of the supper the harper begins to tune and singeth Irish rhymes of ancient making. Supper ended, it is your liberty to sit up or depart to your lodging, you shall have company in both kind. In the morning there will be brought to you a cup of aquavitae [Irish whiskey], it is a very wholesome drink, and natural to digest the crudities of Irish feeding. You may drink a noggin without offense. Breakfast is but a repetition of supper.

François de La Boullaye de la Gouz, writing in 1644, presented a rather starker image:

The castles or houses of the nobility consist of four walls extremely high, thatched with straw; but to tell the truth they are nothing but square towers without windows, or at least having such small apertures as to give no more light than there is in a prison. They have little furniture, and cover their rooms with rushes, of which they make their beds in summer, and of straw in winter. They put the rushes a foot deep on their floors, and on their windows, and many of them ornament the ceilings with branches.

Tower houses were built by people from a broad social spectrum and some were far larger and grander than others. Bunratty Castle, in County Clare (see p. 42), for example, was described by Archbishop Rinuccini, the Papal Nuncio (the pope's representative sent to Ireland in 1645), as 'the most beautiful place I have ever seen. In Italy there is nothing like the palace and grounds of Lord Thomond, with its ponds and parks and three thousand head of deer.'

Towards the end of the medieval period, in the late sixteenth century, there was a move away from these highly defendable, though very uncomfortable, tower houses towards more commodious, better-lit accommodation. A variety of building forms were used, some builders being more progressive than others, and in many instances extensions and modifications were built onto existing tower houses, such as at Donegal Castle (see p. 78).

This wave of building saw a shift away from the compact vertical nature of the tower, towards larger, more rectangular buildings with more elaborate floor plans. Though comfort was important, Ireland was still a turbulent country and defence was not altogether abandoned. The musket had replaced the bow and the new structures often had gun loops and other fortifications to defend entrances. These new buildings are often referred to as fortified houses and can be thought of as the first step away from castles towards country houses. Kanturk Castle, in County Cork is an excellent example (see p. 114).

One distinctive group of castles of this period is the plantation castles of Ulster. In 1607, in what became known as the Flight of the Earls, Hugh O'Neill, Earl of Tyrone, and Rory O'Donnell, Earl of Tyrconnell, along with many of their followers, left Ireland to seek Spanish help to join a rebellion. Their lands in Ulster, comprising about half a million acres, were confiscated and used to plant, or colonise, Ulster with loyal English and Scottish settlers. In exchange for a large grant of land, the settler was required to build a stone castle and bawn. Numerous castles were built, the finest surviving example of which is Monea Castle in County Fermanagh (see p. 182).

By the start of the seventeenth century, the introduction of highly efficient mobile heavy artillery meant that the majority of formerly impregnable castles were now at the mercy of the Elizabethan, and later, the Cromwellian armies. One of Cromwell's tactics was to dismantle a castle after it had been taken. He trained his cannon upon their walls or loaded them with gunpowder, blowing up large holes, to make them of little military use. It is generally recognised that Cromwell's invasion put an end to the building of true castles in Ireland.

Castletown House, County Kildare.

The later years of the seventeenth century, particularly after the definitive Williamite victory at the Boyne, saw massive changes in landownership where the victors, typically the Protestant Anglo-Irish, stripped the losers, typically the Catholic native Irish, of their estates. Tower houses were inconvenient and out-of-date and they were abandoned wholesale.

The eighteenth century saw the heyday of the Irish country house. The Georgian era initially favoured classically styled architecture. The dominant influence was Italian with some of the greatest houses being built in the Palladian style, inspired from the designs of the sixteenth-century Venetian architect, Andrea Palladio. Castletown House, built in 1722 in County Kildare, is a fine example.

Towards the end of the eighteenth century architectural fashion began to turn to the Gothic and the Victorian era saw an architectural revival of the battlements, towers, turrets and arrow loops of medieval castles. The period of unrest leading up to, and after, the 1798 Rebellion, also gave good opportunity to reproduce genuine fortifications. Just as the early eighteenth-century gentleman sought to give up his medieval castle for a Palladian house, the Victorian gentleman spurned his inherited classical mansion and desired a return to the medieval. The possession of a castle signalled status and lineage from long-established families, and the admiration for the neo-Gothic became almost a mania. The leading architects of the late eighteenth and nineteenth centuries, such as John Nash, Francis Johnston, and Sir Richard Morrison, built numerous neo-Gothic castles. A good example is Lough Cutra Castle in County Galway (see p. 158).

The Great Famine, during the middle of the nineteenth century, curtailed the building of new castles and those landowners who had invested in neo-Gothic piles found themselves in considerable financial stress as their tenant farmers failed to pay rent. The Encumbered Estates Court was set up to undertake the sale of bankrupted estates and over the next thirty years, 5 million acres of land changed hands. The land acts of the early twentieth century saw a further dramatic change in landownership when government schemes advanced money to tenants allowing them to buy out their landlord. Many of the aristocracy, clutching their cheques, left Ireland for the more prosperous climes of England, America and Australia. The troubles of the 1920s produced further strife for the typically Protestant, Anglo-Irish owners of large houses and castles. Their allegiance to Britain and also the military use of their properties made them a target for the Irish Republican Army. Numerous neo-Gothic castles were abandoned, a superb example being Kilwaughter Castle in County Antrim (see p. 124).

The Ancient Monuments Protection Act of 1882, an Act of the Parliament of the United Kingdom of Great Britain and Ireland, and the Republic of Ireland National Monuments Act of 1930 form the basis of the protection of historical structures in Ireland. In Northern Ireland, historical structures come under the care of the Department of the Environment, and in the Republic of Ireland, under the care of the Office of Public Works (OPW). Both organisations have performed incredible work restoring, stabilising and opening to the public numerous castles. Excellent examples are Dunluce Castle in County Antrim (see p. 96) and Ross Castle in County Kerry (see p. 192).

Ashford Castle

County Mayo

THE ASHFORD ESTATE was established by the Browne family of Castle Macgarrett, County Mayo, in the first quarter of the eighteenth century. The first house here, Ashford House, a two-storey, five-bay shooting lodge, in the style of a French chateau, was home to Dominic Browne. Dominic inherited and moved into Castle Macgarrett when his father, Geoffrey, died in 1755. In 1814, Ashford was occupied by the Brownes' land agent, Thomas Elwood.

In 1836, Dominic's grandson, also named Dominic, was created Baron Oranmore and Browne in the Irish peerage. He sat as Member of Parliament for County Mayo and spent a fortune campaigning for several elections to ensure his success. One election was said to have cost him £40,000, of which £600 alone went on lemons for whiskey punch. The Great Famine was his final undoing and he was forced to place most of his estates, totalling nearly 8,000 acres, up for sale in the Encumbered Estates Court.

In 1852, Ashford was bought by Benjamin Lee Guinness, the wealthy leader of the Guinness brewing firm. Benjamin was the grandson of Arthur Guinness who had founded the brewery in 1759. Benjamin paid £11,005 for the house and its surrounding 1,179 acres. Captivated by the extreme beauty of the shores of Lough Corrib, Benjamin and his son, Arthur Edward Guinness, went on to buy numerous surrounding estates. These included Rosshill in 1860, the Doon estate with the island ruin of Castle Kirk in 1864, Strandhill in 1871 and several islands and part of the neighbouring Nymphsfield estate in 1875. The Guinness family eventually acquired lands totalling 27,000 acres in County Galway and 4,000 in County Mayo, including thirty-three islands in Lough Corrib and Lough Mask.

Ashford House soon saw vast expansion; the Brownes' chateau was extended and various mock-medieval additions were built, including a five-storey tower house. The estate soon became known as Ashford Castle.

Benjamin was a generous philanthropist who undertook numerous worthy projects. From 1860 to 1865, he set about the restoration of St Patrick's Cathedral in Dublin, an enterprise that cost him over £150,000. In recognition he was made a baronet in 1867. He died in 1868, leaving his estate to his first son, Arthur, who became the second baronet Ashford.

In February 1871, Sir Arthur married Lady Olivia Charlotte Hedges-White, daughter of the third Earl of Bantry, at her father's home, Bantry House in County Cork. Lady Olivia was a passionate historian and antiquary and soon became deeply involved with construction at Ashford Castle. On her marriage she also became the second richest

View from south-west.

Aerial view from north.

woman in both Britain and Ireland; it was said that only Queen Victoria was wealthier.

In 1873, Sir Arthur and Lady Olivia commissioned a large west wing, which was designed initially by James Franklin Fuller, and after the architect-and-client relationship deteriorated, it was completed by George Ashlin. This work connected the extended Browne chateau with a medieval castellated gateway to the west and encased the structure with battlements.

Arthur withdrew from the Guinness company in 1876, selling his half-share to his brother, Edward. Like his father, Arthur was also a very generous philanthropist. His best-known achievement was the purchase, landscaping and then giving to the capital of the central public park of St Stephen's Green in Dublin. In recognition of this and other services to the country, in 1880 he was created Baron Ardilaun, of Ashford in the County of Galway, Ardilaun being the name of one of his islands on Lough Corrib.

Construction continued at Lord Ardilaun's castle, further transforming Ashford to be counted amongst the finest estates in Ireland. The castle saw many more extensions and improvements. The surrounding grounds were developed with walks, gateways, lodges, ramparts and fountains with a water-pumping station. The parkland benefited from the judicious planting of more than a million trees.

Lord Ardilaun found himself threatened in the Land War of the 1880s. Two of his bailiffs were killed in what became known as the Lough Mask Murders. He, however, believed that his massive castellated bridge built over the Cong River would offer him protection from agitated tenants: 'The moat will be protected by battlements, and cannon will be placed at convenient distances. I shall be able to defend myself in case of invasion.'

The Guinness tower, built by
Benjamin Guinness in the forest to
the west of the Ashford in 1864.

While the exterior of Ashford Castle was designed to emulate the impregnable strength of the fortress of a powerful medieval prince, the interior boasted all the opulence, technological improvements and amenities of a great country house. Besides the hall, dining room, library, drawing room, morning room, numerous bedrooms and dressing rooms, there were also a boudoir, smoking room, billiard room, gun room and music room. The domestic offices included a kitchen and sculleries, a pantry, a laundry with separate washing, airing, ironing and folding rooms, separate larders for meat, game and fish, a boot room, still room, brushing room and a silver room.

Lord and Lady Ardilaun entertained lavishly at Ashford. Balls were held during the annual season and a house party was held each year during the week of the Dublin Horse Show. The hospitality offered was truly exceptional and visiting dignitaries included the Prince of Wales (later George V) who visited in 1897 and again in 1905, and Queen Victoria who came to Ashford for dinner in April 1900.

Behind all the entertaining was an army of servants. The census of 1901 shows thirty-eight people employed at the castle. Inside the house there were a housekeeper, cook, butler, under-butler, a lady's maid, two footmen, a still-room maid, scullery maid, kitchen maid and three housemaids; outside the house, there were numerous workers including coachmen, gardeners and labourers.

Lord Ardilaun died in 1915, leaving Ashford in the hands of a family trust. From its purchase by the Guinness family in 1852, more than a million pounds had been spent at Ashford, in today's money approximately €90 million. Lady Ardilaun erected an obelisk in memory of her husband and continued to live at Ashford. Lady Gregory described her as 'a lonely figure in her wealth, childless and feeling the old life shattered around her'.

In 1916, the Congested Districts Board compulsorily purchased the majority of the Guinness's Connacht estate for £50,000. It amounted to 2,000 acres in County Mayo and almost 28,000 acres in County Galway. Lady Ardilaun eventually gave up on Ashford and the castle went to her husband's nephew, the Hon. Ernest Guinness. She then took up residence at another Guinness property, St Anne's, a 500-acre estate on the north side of Dublin. As St Anne's became increasingly dilapidated and its gardens fell into decay, Lady Ardilaun would escape the cold and damp winters by moving into the Shelbourne Hotel, Dublin, with her maid and secretary. She died in December 1925, at the age of seventy-five.

Ernest Guinness frequently joked that far too many people were employed at Ashford, 'every one of whom might fall over if you removed his sweeping brush'. Relations with his staff gradually deteriorated to the point that in the summer of 1938 they went on strike, looking for a wage increase of two shillings a week. The story goes that he became so exasperated by their behaviour that he left Ashford in his private plane and never returned.

In 1939, Ashford Castle and its entire contents were sold at an auction that lasted for two weeks. The Irish government purchased the castle and leased it and 170 surrounding acres to the hotelier Noel Huggard. Thereafter Ashford has operated as one of Ireland's leading five-star country hotels. In 1970, the hotel was bought by John Mulcahy, who oversaw its restoration, doubling its size with the addition of a new wing, and further developing the grounds and gardens with a golf course. The hotel changed hands again in 1985, 2007 and again in 2013 when €47 million was spent on its restoration.

Ashford Castle consistently wins many national and international awards and is voted amongst the world's top hotels. (www.ashfordcastle.com)

Aughnanure
Castle

County Galway

Aerial view from east.

THIS WELL-PRESERVED TOWER HOUSE was once the stronghold of the ferocious O'Flaherty clan. The O'Flahertys' territory included most of *Iar-Connacht*, a huge stretch of land that extended from the mouth of the Galway River, along the western banks of Lough Corrib, right up to the shores of the Atlantic.

Aughnanure was built at a highly defensive position where the Drimneed River once ran along three sides of the castle, forming a natural barrier. The river also provided an access route downstream to Lough Corrib and on to Galway city, where the O'Flahertys harassed, robbed and threatened its Anglo-Norman citizens. Galway endured difficult relations with many of its Irish neighbours and a bye-law stated that 'neither O' nor Mac shall strutte nor swagger through the streets of Galway'. This forbade the native Irish, whose surnames mostly began with an O' or a Mac, to enter the town. The O'Flahertys seem to have been particularly feared and a gate erected at the west end of the town bore the inscription 'From the Ferocious O'Flahertys, may God protect us.'

There may have been an earlier wooden or earthen defensive structure at Aughnanure, though no evidence of this survives. There is also no record of a definite construction date of the stone castle that stands on the site today, though it is thought to originate from the early years of the sixteenth century.

The tower house rises six storeys above a battered or sloping base. The angle of this battered base was designed to deflect horizontally objects thrown from above into the path of attacking forces. On the eastern side of the tower, a decorative doorway is protected by a machicolation high above, from where arrows, stones or other missiles could be fired down on unwelcome visitors. Bartizans at the second-floor level on the north-east and south-east corners also provided projecting defensive positions with gun loops for muskets. Just inside the tower doorway, a murder hole in the ceiling allowed the defenders to shoot arrows or drop boiling oil on anyone who managed to enter. A guards' office to the right of the entrance housed men who controlled access up the tower house via a stone spiral staircase that rises in the south-east corner. The rest of the ground floor was used as a storeroom and servants' sleeping area. There are stone vaulted ceilings between the ground and first floors, and also between the third and fourth floors. The remainder of the floors are supported by wooden beams. On the third floor, a grand fireplace indicates that this may well have housed the lord's chamber, and on the fourth floor a trapdoor gives access to a concealed room. The top floor, re-covered with a beautifully crafted oak roof, is probably where the O'Flahertys held court. Above the roofline a wall walk provided a fine view over the surrounding countryside.

The tower house was, unusually, surrounded by both an inner and outer bawn. The walls of the inner bawn along the riverside still survive, though the rest are no longer present. A flanking circular turret, later reused as a dovecote, marks the south-east corner of the inner bawn. Further to the south-east, the outer bawn walls were defended by five flanking turrets and enclosed an area measuring about 46 by 49 metres. To the south-west, another wall marks the site of the castle's once splendid banqueting hall. Two surviving windows in this wall are beautifully decorated with carvings including depictions of vine leaves and grapes.

The epithets, or nicknames, of various O'Flaherty leaders suggest there was little peace with their neighbours in Galway city. Donal 'an Chogaidh', or 'of the Wars', was the head of the clan and lived at Aughnanure. He was married to the notorious Gráinne (Grace) O'Malley (also known as Granuaile or Gráinne Mhaol). Another member of the O'Flaherty clan, Murrough 'na dTuadh' ('of the Battle-axes') frequently mounted raids on the English around Galway. In 1564, at

(L–r): Banqueting hall window, with elaborate carvings at top; view into third-floor chamber with grand fireplace at rear.

Third-floor chamber with staircase at rear right; the fourth floor was timber (note the joist holes in the walls).

Looking down the spiral staircase in south-east corner.

EXPLORING IRELAND'S CASTLES

Top floor, with a view of the new, beautifully crafted oak rafters.

Traban, a beach about three kilometres west of Galway, Murrough decisively defeated an English force sent to capture him. A few years later he accepted a pardon for various offences and was appointed by Queen Elizabeth I as chieftain of the territory of Iar-Connacht, despite Donal still being the legitimate clan leader. The angry Donal rose up against the queen, but was betrayed by Murrough, who sent warning of his rebellion to the English. Sir Edward Fitton, President of Connacht, soon marched against Aughnanure, where Donal found his castle no match for the English artillery. For the only time in its long existence, the castle fell to the enemy force. Fitton subsequently rewarded Murrough by presenting him with the captured castle. Murrough added to its defences and lived here until his death in 1593.

Donal of the Wars died soon after losing the castle, and his wife, Gráinne, returned to her O'Malley homeland in County Mayo, taking with her many O'Flaherty followers who were loyal to her. Here she gained her famous reputation as 'The Pirate Queen of Connacht'.

In 1618, King James I granted Aughnanure to Hugh O'Flaherty, but by the middle of the seventeenth century the castle had been confiscated from the O'Flahertys and given to the Marquess of Clanrickarde. Clanrickarde wrote a number of letters from the castle in his campaign against the Cromwellian forces at that time. By 1687, he had let the castle back to the O'Flahertys for an annual rent of £76. In 1719, Bryan O'Flaherty took out a mortgage of £1,600 to purchase the castle, borrowing the money from Lord Saint George. When the mortgage was not repaid, Saint George took possession of the castle but by the 1850s it was again back in the hands of the O'Flahertys. About this time Edmund O'Flaherty planted yew trees around the castle in honour of its original name and from where Aughnanure is derived, in Irish a*chadh na n-Iubhar* or 'the field of the yews'.

In 1952, Peter O'Flaherty handed the castle over to the Irish state. It is now in the care of the OPW and open to the public daily from March to November.

Ballyadams Castle

County Laois

19

Ground-floor entrance.

THE TOWNLAND OF BALLYADAMS was known anciently as Kylmehyde and an early fortification was recorded here in 1346, though no evidence of this edifice remains.

In the latter part of the fifteenth century, Adam O'More built a castle here, and the townland became known as Ballyadams (or Town of Adam). This is the six-storey medieval tower house forming the central section of the present ruined castle of Ballyadams. In 1546, it was the stronghold of Gilla-Patrick O'More, Chief of Laois.

The tower, which survives in excellent condition, has rounded corners at the south-west and north-west, between which is an imposing entranceway. The entranceway is recessed and covered with a round segmental arch containing a murder hole, from where boiling oil or other objects could be thrown down on an attacking army. Another segmental arch near the upper storey forms a machicolation over the entrance, from where similar objects could also be thrown, or arrows fired down.

There is a winding stone staircase in the north-west corner of the tower, leading to the upper floors and to the summit, at a height of about 25 metres. The interior of the tower is full of small rooms and dark recesses. The ground floor forms a D-shaped room with a vaulted roof. A rectangular hole in the floor leads to an oubliette or prison below. The first floor has two barrel-vaulted rooms, and the second floor a larger chamber that had a wooden ceiling. The fourth floor probably contained the main sleeping chamber for the castle's occupants, with the fifth floor giving access to a wall walk and a small lookout tower.

Attached to the east side of the tower are the ruins of a large, rectangular, fortified three-storey house. Parts of this house may have been built at the same time as or shortly after the tower, with further extensive alterations occurring in the eighteenth century, including the insertion of large windows. The remains of a wing can be seen on the west side of the tower, which were also constructed later than the central tower, and may never have been completed. There is also some evidence of a bawn, which may have enclosed an area south of the castle.

Following the rebellion of Gilla-Patrick O'More in 1546, the O'Mores and O'Connors burned the town of Athy. Sir Anthony St Leger, Lord Deputy of Ireland, and the Earl of Desmond soon took a large force into Laois to quench the disturbance and take Ballyadams Castle and the county of Laois for the British Crown. By 1549, a Welsh man, John Bowen, was constable of the castle. Given the nickname Shane-a-Feeka or 'John of the Pike', he was a cruel and brutal man who always carried a pike on his ventures. He died in 1569, and was succeeded by his son Robert, Sheriff of Laois in 1570. Robert's son, John, was knighted on 13 November 1629 and was Provost Marshal of Leinster and Meath.

Panoramic interior view of first floor.

(L–r) View down from fifth floor; view to tower from remains of attached fortified house.

View south-east from roof.

Spiral staircase in north-west corner (looking down).

In 1643, the Catholic Confederates under Lord Castlehaven were attacking Graham Castle, nearby at Ballylinan. Lord Castlehaven knew Sir John Bowen and visited Ballyadams to insist that the Catholic Confederates also place a garrison in Ballyadams to fight the English Parliamentarian army. Bowen flatly refused and, calling his family around him, told Castlehaven that he would place his own two beautiful daughters on chairs hanging high on the castle's walls, so they would be killed if Castlehaven tried to take the castle by force. Castlehaven soon backed down and the castle and the Bowens were saved. This incident is recorded at length in the Irish ballad, 'The Romance of Ballyadams'.

The antiquarian Austin Cooper visited the castle on 10 August 1782 and made the following entry in his diary: 'The inside of the castle exhibits a scene sufficient to excite compassion from every lover of ancient grandeur – the boarded floors all torn up, the plastered walls and ceilings threatening the observer with destruction, and, to complete this grand scene of desolation, the great state room still remains hung with elegant tapestry now left to rot away.'

The current owner of the castle and surrounding land is a direct descendant of Pierce Butler who married Katherine Bowen, heiress of the castle who lived here in the latter years of the seventeenth century.

Mr Garrett Butler was the last of the Butlers to inhabit the castle and retired to County Tipperary following the 1798 Rebellion. Captain Robert McLean, a Scotsman, occupied the castle for a time and was gamekeeper to the Kemmis family who took ownership of Ballyadams in the 1840s. In 1896, the Ballyadams estate was sold to various tenants. McLean and his son-in-law, William Shore, purchased the castle and some surrounding land, replacing the old tower roof with corrugated iron, before abandoning the castle a few years later.

In 1910, the castle was the scene of a strange invasion, when two bullocks managed to climb the circular staircase, one entering the room on the first floor, while the other climbed all the way to the roof where it got stuck beside the battlements. The owner feared the animal would jump and sent for a butcher from Athy. Locals, however, managed to secure it with ropes and somehow it was safely returned to the ground.

Ballyadams Castle is private property and is not open to the public.

Barryscourt
Castle

County Cork ~

View of towerhouse from east.

BARRYSCOURT CASTLE IS LOCATED about a kilometre south of Carrigtwohill in County Cork. The story goes that a stone found on the site was inscribed 'O Lehan hoc Fecit MCIII', indicating that the O'Lehane family had some kind of structure here, possibly an ecclesiastical building, in 1103. There is no trace of this stone today and the castle that now stands on the site dates from the fifteenth century when it was built by the Barry family.

Philip de Barri arrived in Ireland in 1183, and his son, William, had lands in east Cork and Cork Harbour granted to him by King John in 1206. In 1490, the head of the Barry family was summoned to Parliament as Lord Barry of Barry's Court. By the sixteenth century the Barrys had divided into three sections: Barrymore, the head of the family who lived in Barryscourt; the Barry Roe, or Red Barrys, who ruled from Timoleague; and the Barry Oges, or junior Barrys, who had lands at Innishannon and Kinsale.

In the 1550s, James Fitz Richard Barry Roe succeeded to the titles Baron Barry and Viscount Buttevant by murdering his cousins, Redmond and John. Two other cousins, Richard and David, fled and sought refuge with the Earl of Desmond. James' violent life eventually caught up with him and he was arrested in 1579 on suspicion of involvement in the Desmond uprising. He was imprisoned in Dublin Castle where he died in 1581, before his trial took place.

Sir Walter Raleigh took a fancy to Barryscourt, describing the castle as 'a great strength in the country and a safety to all passengers between Youghal and Cork'. After James' death the castle was granted to Raleigh. James' son, David Barry, fifth Viscount Buttevant, reacted violently and set fire to the castle before giving it up, making it of little use to its new owner.

David Barry predicted the collapse of the Desmond cause and changed sides, submitting to the English Crown in order to save his estate. His submission was accepted, and although he contrived to continue a Catholic, he remained a Royalist for the rest of his life. Barryscourt was returned to him and he did considerable rebuilding, recording the

First-floor chamber. Note evidence of original pointed vaulted ceiling at rear.

North end of second-floor chamber. Note unpainted stripe on the wall where the original ceiling would have been.

Second-floor chamber with fireplace commissioned by David Barry in 1588.

date on an inscription on a fireplace in the second-storey of the castle, 'A.D. 1588. I.H.S D.B. ETE. R. ME FIERI FECERVT', meaning 'in the year of our Lord 1588, Jesus Saviour, David Barry and Ellen Roche caused me to be made.

David died at Barryscourt in 1617 and was succeeded by his grandson David FitzDavid Barry, sixth Viscount Buttevant, who had been brought up a Protestant and firmly sided with the English. He married Lady Alice, the eldest daughter of Richard Boyle, first Earl of Cork, and this marriage helped him in becoming elevated to the title Earl of Barrymore in 1628. Barryscourt was seemingly an unfitting residence for an earl and the old castle was mortgaged to his father-in-law, and a new fortified mansion built at Castlelyons.

Successive members of the Barry family increasingly spent more time in England and turned into absentee landlords of the worst kind. In 1751, Richard Barry became the sixth earl when he was just six years old. Living in London he became a reckless gambler and drinker, served briefly in the 9th Regiment of Dragoons before dying of a fever at the age of twenty-eight. His son, also named Richard Barry, became the seventh earl when he was just five. He became an infamous rake, gambler, sportsman and womaniser, gaining the nicknames 'Hellgate' and 'the Rake of Rakes'.

On 9 November 1791, he mortgaged his Irish property for £130,000, about €15 million in today's money. Remarkably, the entire sum was quickly wasted. He lived fast and died at the young age of just twenty-four. Whilst riding in a carriage, a loaded gun he was carrying was accidentally discharged, shooting him in the eye. In his brief life he had squandered the entire family fortune, more than £300,000 or about €34 million in today's money.

After the Barrys' departure to Castlelyons, Barryscourt was let to the Coppinger family who built a farmhouse alongside it. The property later passed to the O'Connell Bianconi family, though the castle had long been unoccupied, its basement being used as a granary.

Barryscourt Castle comprises a large, rectangular main block, measuring about 14 by 11 metres, with projecting towers on three corners. The original entrance was probably via external timber steps leading to the first floor of the castle. In the sixteenth century this was changed to the ground-floor arched doorway at the north end of the east wall, which is still used today.

Inside the doorway a small lobby gives access to the main ground-floor chamber, and also to a steep mural staircase that leads to the first and second floors. The first-floor chamber has a barrel-vaulted roof, though it was once covered by a pointed vault, evidence of which survives at the south end. The main second-floor chamber measures about 12 by 6 metres and contains the fireplace on the west wall that was commissioned by David Barry in 1588. Spiral stairs at the east end of the south wall give entry to two higher chambers and a wall walk. The castle's corner towers also contain various mural and garderobe chambers.

Outside the castle, to the north-east, there is a bawn with towers on the south-east, north-east and north-west corners. Some of the bawn walls were lowered and altered to accommodate eighteenth-century farm buildings; just outside is the two-storey farmhouse built by the Coppingers.

Barryscourt fell increasingly into dereliction during the twentieth century until 1988, when the Barryscourt Trust, an Irish-American Foundation, was formed to develop the castle as a cultural and tourist centre. In the early 1990s the President of Ireland, Mary Robinson, visited the castle to launch a restoration project. The castle, its interior, and grounds have all be magnificently restored and are today open to the public by the OPW in conjunction with the Barryscourt Trust.

Birr Castle

County Offaly

THE FIRST CASTLE AT BIRR was the 'Black Castle', a medieval stronghold of the O'Carroll clan, powerful Irish chieftains who ruled over the surrounding territory of Ely, and termed themselves Princes of Ely. Despite various submissions and treaties with the English Crown, the O'Carrolls were continually fighting amongst themselves, with the neighbouring clan, the Molloys, as well as with the English forces. By the early seventeenth century numerous murders and assassinations had left four different branches of the O'Carrolls disputing leadership, and the region was in chaos. In 1619, the death of Sir Charles O'Carroll gave the English an opportunity for the Commission for the Plantation of Ely O'Carroll to declare the territory Crown property, and introduce English settlers in an effort to promote stability.

William and Laurence Parsons came from England to Ireland in about 1590. William, the elder brother, rose quickly through various offices, becoming Surveyor General of Ireland; Commissioner of the Plantations; Supervisor and Extender of Crown Lands, Master of the Irish Court of Wards; and Lord Justice of the Kingdom. He was created a baronet in 1620. Laurence, the younger brother, was a lawyer who was also quickly promoted, becoming Clerk of the Crown, Attorney General for Munster, Judge of the Admiralty, deputy Vice Admiral for Munster and Second Baron of the Irish Exchequer. He was knighted in 1620. These positions gave both brothers ample opportunity for building up large landed estates. In 1620, Laurence acquired 1,000 acres of arable land and 277 of wood and bog from the O'Carrolls' territory, centred on the town and castle of Birr. On 26 June of that year, his new estate was constituted a manor under the new name of Parsonstown.

Under Sir Laurence Parsons, the town flourished. The main street was immaculately paved and a fine demanded from anyone who 'cast any dunge rubbidge filth or sweepings into the forestreet'. Fires were to be lit only in houses with a stone chimney or the occupier would otherwise be banished from the town, and women were forbidden to serve beer 'uppon payne to bee sett in the stocks by the constable for 3 whole markett dayes'. Sir Laurence also started a glass factory under a Huguenot family, the Bigos, who soon supplied the upper classes of Dublin with their window and table glass. The town's growing prosperity was further elevated with two weekly markets.

Sir Laurence enlarged the O'Carroll castle, rebuilding a gatehouse that stood to the south-east. In subsequent years the O'Carroll castle would be entirely demolished and the gatehouse vastly enlarged, incorporating two flanking towers, to become the present castle.

When Sir Laurence died in 1628 he was succeeded by his sons Richard and then William. In 1642, William defended the castle against an attack by the Irish rebels. Birr was besieged again in January 1643, and this time the castle was captured and garrisoned by the Confederate Catholics. In 1650, the Parliamentarians under General Ireton recaptured the castle but the Catholic forces set fire to it before leaving. After the war, Sir William's son, another Laurence, returned to the castle and rebuilt it. This Laurence was created a baronet in 1677.

In 1681, Thomas Dineley, an English topographer, recorded the following about Birr in his diary: 'Lord of this town is Sir Laurence Parsons, where there is much plenty of Ewe-Timber, that of his House the Windows, Staircases, Window Cases, Tables, Chairs, Benches, and Stooles are formed therewith. Here is sayd to be the fairest staircase in Ireland.' The staircase still survives, though it was partly rebuilt after a fire in 1832.

In 1690, the castle again came under attack, this time by the Jacobite army under the Duke of Berwick. Those inside the castle were reduced to making their own ammunition by melting down a huge lead tank previously used by the cook for salting beef. During the assault, three Jacobite cannonballs smashed through the parlour window, two of them becoming stuck in an internal wall. Numerous other cannonballs hit the northern side of the castle, but did not breach its walls. When the Jacobites eventually left, marching on for Limerick, the castle was used by the Williamites for some months as a military hospital.

Birr was left in peace for the majority of the eighteenth century and little is recorded at the castle until 1778, when Sir William Parsons demolished the old O'Carroll castle and its adjoining stables, kitchen and courtyard, replacing them with the great lawn that lies in front of the castle today. Sir William also began to plant many shrubs and trees, dredge the lake and develop the surrounding parkland in a style inspired by Lancelot 'Capability' Brown.

The inner gatehouse that separates the castle from its parkland.

In 1806, Sir William's son, another Laurence, became the second Earl of Rosse, inheriting the title from his uncle. He wished to transform the castle into a seat befitting his title and began by making a series of sketches of medieval rearrangements before employing the services of a little-known local architect, John Johnston. The front façade was refaced and Gothicised, an impressive entrance was added and a single-storey extension built at the end of the castle above the River Camcor. This extension houses the music room, a dramatic Gothic marvel with its elaborate plaster vaulting and huge tracery windows. In 1832, after a fire damaged the roof, the central block was given an extra storey, complete with a battlemented roofline.

The third Earl of Rosse took Birr in a different direction. Educated at home and then at Trinity College, Dublin, he went on to graduate in mathematics with first-class honours at Oxford. He was MP for King's County (County Offaly) but resigned his seat in 1834 to devote his time to scientific concerns. He built a series of telescopes, starting with a telescope with a 15-inch (38 cm) parabolic mirror, moving up to a 36-inch (91 cm) in 1839 and finishing with the 72-inch (180 cm) mirrored 'Leviathan' in 1843.

Constructed in a stone battlemented and turreted building beside the castle, the 16-ton Leviathan remained the world's largest telescope until 1917, and enabled Rosse to discover and catalogue numerous nebulas and galaxies. In its day, the Leviathan was the only telescope in the world capable of seeing the spiral shape of galaxies and this attracted astronomers from across the globe. Birr soon became an international scientific centre and publications flowed through various scientific journals of the day, including the Royal Irish Academy and Royal Astronomical Society. The third Earl became President of the Royal Society from 1849 to 1854, and received its Royal Medal in 1851. He became a Knight of St Patrick in 1845 and Chancellor of Trinity College, Dublin in 1862. Correspondence with several Russian scientists led to him being elected a member of the Imperial Academy of St Petersburg in 1853 and Napoleon III created him a Knight of the Legion of Honour in 1855.

The third Earl's wife, Lady Mary, assisted in many astronomical discoveries and was also an accomplished early pioneer of photography. In 1859, she won the first Silver Medal awarded by the Photographic Society of Ireland. An extensive darkroom was installed in Birr Castle and is the oldest surviving example of its kind in the world.

View of the castle from north-west.

During the Great Famine (1845–1852), local employment was provided to over 500 men on the land that surrounds the castle. The lake and demesne walls were enlarged and Lady Rosse's uncle, Colonel Richard Wharton Myddleton, designed the massive star-shaped ramparts that separate the castle from its parkland.

Laurence, the fourth Earl, continued the astronomical tradition, drawing the first map of the moon's surface, and also measuring its radiant heat. The second son, Clere, became a highly successful railway engineer. The third son, Randal, chose a non-scientific career, becoming a canon of the Church of England. The fourth son, Charles, became world-famous as the inventor of the steam turbine. Parsons turbines were installed in numerous British and American naval warships and Cunard express passenger liners, as well as the world's first turbine power stations. His company eventually became part of Rolls-Royce and still survives as a division of Siemens.

Subsequent members of the Parsons family were devoted to developing the 150 acres of gardens at Birr. The fifth Earl flattened the moat between the castle and the river to make terraces, and planted fine trees and shrubs along the banks of the Camcor, including a collection purchased from the world-renowned Veitch nursery following its 1914 closure. The sixth Earl, a renowned horticulturalist and plantsman, gathered many rare specimens from the Himalaya and the Far East, and started the great collection of magnolias. His wife, Lady Anne, planted the romantic hornbeam cloister walk, with the world's tallest box hedges, to celebrate their marriage in 1935.

The seventh and present Earl of Rosse, Brendan Parsons, and his wife, Alison, Lady Rosse, have visited many countries on plant-collecting expeditions, including Kyrgyzstan, Pakistan, Iran, South Africa, New Zealand, China and Bhutan.

Today the gardens at Birr are among the most famous in Ireland. They are open to the public daily, along with the science centre located in the castle courtyard. Birr Castle itself remains the family home of the Parsons and is open to the public by guided tour during the months of May, June, July and August. (www.birrcastle.com)

Blarney Castle

County Cork

View of tower house from south.

There is a stone there whoever kisses, oh! he never misses to grow eloquent,
'Tis he may clamber to a lady's chamber, or become a member of Parliament.
A clever spouter, he'll sure turn out, or an out-and-outer to be let alone,
Don't hope to hinder him or bewilder him. Sure he's a pilgrim from the Blarney Stone!

– Francis Sylvester Mahony (Father Prout) in his *Reliques* of 1860.

THE BLARNEY STONE, located high in the battlements of Blarney Castle, has made the castle the most famous in Ireland, if not the world, with its name having passed into the English language as a noun meaning smooth and flattering or cajoling talk. This derives from the legend that tells that those who kiss it will be given the gift of eloquence.

Crofton Croker, the early nineteenth-century antiquarian, wrote that Cormac mac Diarmada, Chief of the Mac Carthaigh Mhúscraighe (Lord of Muskerry) was instructed by Queen Elizabeth I's agents to renounce his Irish customs and become a good and loyal English subject. He procrastinated and made promises 'with soft words and fair speech' time and time again, until the queen burst out with the famous words, 'This is all Blarney, what he says he never means!'

There are several other versions of the story to explain the mysterious power of the stone, such as it originating in the Middle East, where it was none other than the pillow upon which Jacob's head was resting when he had his famous dream, or that it is actually part of the Lia Fáil (Stone of Scone), given to one MacCarthy lord for helping Edward the Bruce of Scotland. It is worth pointing out that the actual stone is also the subject of some dispute. Tourists today line

View to tower
house entrance.

39

View into the family room (lower) and the great hall above. The dividing timber floor is no longer present.

up on the castle battlements to lean out over a plummeting edge to kiss the sill stone of one of the machicolations, supposedly damaged in Cromwell's time. Other candidates for the stone were a water-worn hollow stone situated on the parapet of the east side of the turret that disappeared in the late 1700s, a stone bearing the date 1703 on the highest part of the north-east angle, or another stone engraved with a shamrock. Whatever the origins of the story or the actual stone, the tourism industry in Cork has been blessing it ever since.

Tradition has it that the castle was built in 1446 by Cormac Láidir MacCarthy, though as the MacCarthys seemingly did not gain possession of Blarney until the 1480s, it is more likely that it actually comprises a narrow tower built by the Lombard family, which was extended by the MacCarthys with the addition of a large tower house in the late fifteenth or early sixteenth century. Blarney then became the chief stronghold of the MacCarthys, who had an army of more than 3,000 men.

In 1628, Charles Oge MacCarthy was created Baron of Blarney and Viscount Muskerry. In 1658, the second Viscount, Donnchadh (or Donough), was raised with the title Earl of Clancarty. The brother of the fourth Earl of Clancarty, the Hon. Justin MacCarthy, was created Viscount Mountcashel and both brothers were supporters of James II. As a result of the Williamite victories at Boyne and Aughrim, the family's titles and estates were declared forfeit in 1691.

Donough, the fourth Earl of Clancarty, was captured and imprisoned in the Tower of London. He made a resourceful escape and ended up living on a small island in the River Elbe, near Hamburg. According to legend, before

(L–r): View from the battlements into the interior; the famous Blarney stone (centre rear of barred opening).

leaving Blarney he packed all his silver and valuables into a chest that was thrown into the castle lake. Here his ghost rises every seven years in the hope that someone will return his lost treasure. Another version goes that as soon as the estate is restored to the MacCarthys the chest will be discovered.

The Blarney estate was purchased by the Hollow Sword Blades Company, an English firm that diversified from sword manufacturing into land purchase. They let the castle to Rowland Davies, Dean of Cork. When Sir Richard Pyne, Lord Chief Justice of Ireland, bought the castle in 1703, Davies apparently took away many of its ancient oak beams for his new residence at Dawstown, County Cork. Within a few months Pyne sold the castle to Sir James Jefferyes who had been appointed Governor of Cork in 1698.

Sir James spent the remainder of his life at Blarney. His grandson, James St John Jefferyes, embarked on an ambitious scheme of improvements of the estate and also the commercial development of both castle and nearby village. He built a late Georgian Gothic mansion against the east side of the old castle that is shown in an engraving in the 1817 book *Narrative of a Residence in Ireland* by Anne Plumptre. James St John also laid out beautiful ornamental gardens that became much admired by painters and poets. He transformed Blarney village from two or three mud cabins to a commercial centre with ninety houses, mills and weaving halls for linen manufacture. It also appears that it was about this time that the legend of kissing the Blarney Stone began to spread to all corners of the world.

In 1789, Charles Étienne Coquebert de Montbret, the French Consul in Dublin, gave an account thus: 'Blarney Castle on the top of which is a large stone that visitors who climb up are made to kiss, with a promise that in so doing they will gain the privilege of telling lies for seven years.'

James St John's mansion was destroyed by fire in 1820 and today all that survives is the tall circular tower that stands beside the castle. In 1846, Blarney passed from the Jefferyes to the Colthurst families with the marriage of Louisa Jane Jefferyes to Sir George Conway Colthurst. In 1874, a new house was built about 200 metres south of the old castle. Named Blarney House, it was built in the Scots Baronial style, to the designs of Sir Thomas Lanyon, with pinnacles, crow-stepped gables and a profusion of turrets with conical roofs.

The Blarney estate remains in the hands of the Colthurst family, with Sir Charles St John Colthurst currently at the helm. Blarney Castle and its surrounding parkland are open to the public year round and are one of the most popular tourist destinations in Munster. Blarney House, still home to the Colthursts, is also open to visitors during the summer months. (www.blarneycastle.ie)

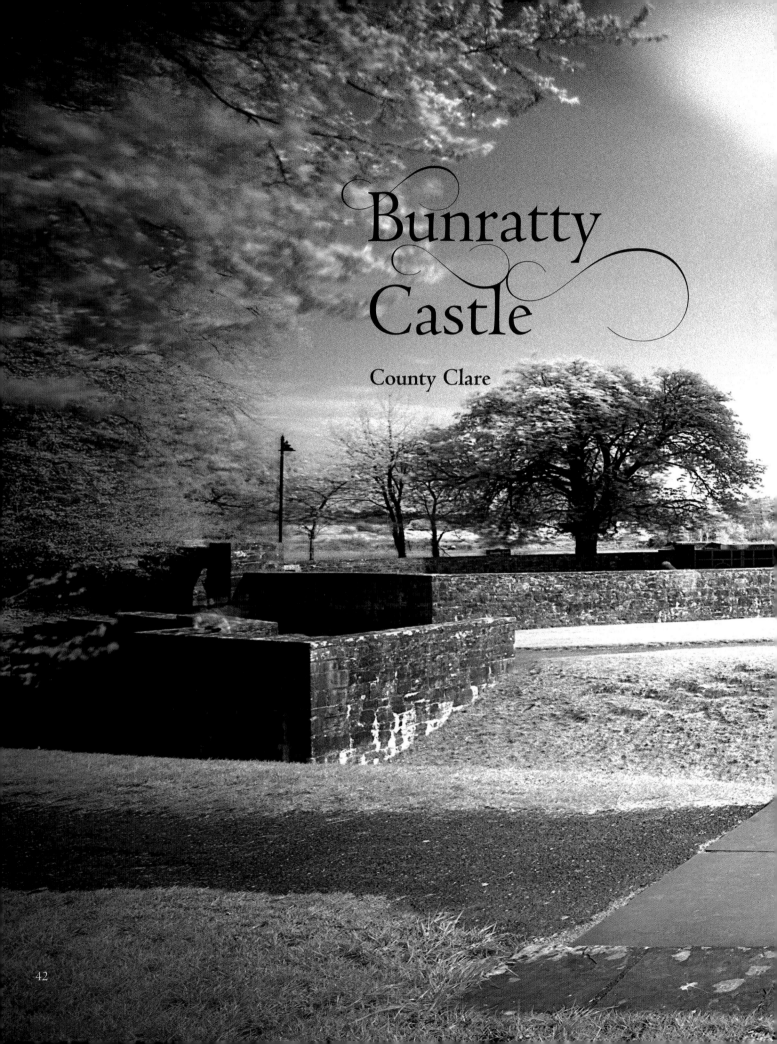

Bunratty Castle

County Clare

Photograph by George Macnamara (c. 1910).

BUNRATTY CASTLE DERIVES ITS NAME from the Irish '*bun Ráite*', meaning 'mouth of the Ratty', relating to its position where the River Ratty joins the Shannon Estuary. This position has long been of significant strategic importance, being a controlling point for access from the Shannon to Limerick city.

The first settlement here is thought to have been a Viking camp, set up by the Norseman as a base for their plundering and pillaging raids up the Shannon. Tradition relates that by the end of the tenth century Brian Boru had attacked the Vikings through the cover of Cratloe Woods and destroyed their camp.

In 1248, King Henry III granted Bunratty and the surrounding district of Tradree to Robert de Muscegros. Muscegros was charged an annual rent of £30, but was pardoned this rent for two years, and also allowed to cut down 200 oak trees from Cratloe forest, in order to build a castle at Bunratty. Muscegros Castle was the first of four castles to be built at Bunratty. No evidence of it has been found, though it almost certainly comprised a typical Norman motte and bailey, where a wooden palisade and ditch surrounded a raised earthen mound, topped with a wooden keep.

Muscegros held his castle for a relatively short period, the land being taken back by King Henry in the early 1270s. In 1276, Henry's successor, Edward I, granted the lordship of Thomond, an area which covered most of Counties Clare and Limerick as well as parts of County Tipperary, to the Anglo-Norman Thomas de Clare. He based himself at Bunratty and set about building a stone castle on, or near, the site of the present castle. Comprising a large single stone tower, its walls were painted lime white.

The O'Briens, descendants of Brian Boru and a major force in Thomond from the earliest times, strongly opposed de Clare, attacking his castle numerous times. In 1284, while de Clare was in England, the castle was captured and destroyed. He rebuilt it in 1287 and managed to hold off the O'Briens until 1318. That year both Thomas de Clare and his son, Richard, were killed in battle. Lady de Clare set fire to the castle to prevent its reuse and fled to Limerick.

By the fourteenth century, Limerick city had become an increasingly important port for the English Crown. In 1353 a new castle, the third at Bunratty, was built to guard against attacks along the Shannon by the native Irish. Its construction, however, had hardly been completed before it was captured. Its governor, Thomas Fitzjohn Fitzmaurice, spent some time in Limerick prison, charged with letting the castle fall into the hands of Murtough O'Brien.

Construction of the fourth castle was started in the middle of the fifteenth century by the chief of the MacNamara clan, Maccon Sioda, and completed by his son, Sean Fionn, who died in 1467. Their castle, which still stands today, comprises a massive three-storey central block with square five-storey towers projecting at each corner. The southern and northern towers are joined by a high, wide arch.

By 1500, the castle had passed into the hands of the O'Briens, probably through the marriage of Sean Fionn's daughter, Raghnailt, to Turlogh O'Brien, Prince of Thomond. Turlogh and Raghnailt's son, Murrough, surrendered to Henry VIII in 1542. Giving up his lands and Gaelic loyalty, he swore allegiance to the English Crown, and in return was regranted his lands and the title Earl of Thomond. The O'Briens relocated from their castle in Ennis and made Bunratty their chief stronghold.

Donogh, the fourth Earl of Thomond, known as the 'Great Earl', fought with the English against the Irish, and in return received an annual pension of £200 for life. In the latter part of the sixteenth century he made many improvements to the castle, including replacing the roof with lead, inserting stained-glass windows and fine chimney pieces, as well as decorating the ceilings with elaborate scroll and floral stucco-work. Some of this stucco decoration survives in the chapel in the south-east tower and also in the Great Hall. This magnificent hall was where the Great

The lower hall, laid out for the twice-nightly medieval banquet.

View from the solar into the Great Hall.

(L–r) North solar (the earl's family's private living quarters); The earl's bedroom.

Earl received his formal visitors. It measures about 10 by 15 metres and rises to a height of nearly 15 metres. There are no fireplaces or chimneys; instead a fire was lit in a brazier in the centre of the room, with the smoke escaping through a louvre in the roof. The current roof was replaced by the OPW, which modelled it on the medieval roof of Dunsoghly Castle in County Dublin. Flights of steps in the north-east and north-west towers ran to the earl's apartments which included the solar (a private area for the earl and his family) where a hatch overlooks the Great Hall, a private chapel and bedchamber. Below the Great Hall is another hall where the castle soldiers lived, slept and ate. It is now where tourists dine on medieval banquets, which are served twice a night all year round.

Archbishop Rinuccini, the Papal Nuncio, visited the sixth Earl of Thomond in 1646, during his visit to Ireland. He described Bunratty as 'the most beautiful place I have ever seen. In Italy there is nothing like the palace and grounds of Lord Thomond, with its ponds and parks and three thousand head of deer.'

Bunratty remained in the hands of the O'Briens until 1712, when Henry, the eighth and last Earl of Thomond sold the castle and 472 acres of land to Thomas Amory for £225 and an annual rent of £120. Amory occupied the castle for a few years, before selling it to Thomas Studdert *c.* 1720. The Studderts lived in a seventeenth-century house that nestled against the castle walls until 1804, when they built Bunratty House, about a kilometre north of the castle. The castle was left to fall into disrepair. Around the middle of the nineteenth century it was used as a barracks by the Royal Irish Constabulary and about 1850 a strange discovery was made by workmen repairing a floor. Some slabs were removed, revealing a large chamber, the walls of which were hung with brocaded silk. In the centre of the room was a skeleton, beside which lay a long, silver knife. The chamber had neither door nor window, nor any apparent means of entrance.

In the late nineteenth century the roof of the Great Hall collapsed, after which the castle was completely abandoned.

In 1953, the ruined castle was brought by the seventh Viscount Gort, Standish Prendergast Vereker. Encouraged by a group of friends, including the antique dealer and medievalist John Hunt, Lord Gort set about restoring Bunratty Castle in partnership with the OPW and Bord Fáilte. When its restoration was complete, Gort and Hunt began filling the castle's rooms with medieval furniture and art. These were acquired from abroad as no Irish pieces had survived the turbulent medieval period.

Bunratty Castle was opened to the public in 1960 and held its first medieval banquet, run by Shannon Development, in 1963. Today the castle forms the centrepiece of the Bunratty Folk Park, a tourist attraction operated by Shannon Heritage that draws over 600,000 visitors annually. (www.shannonheritage.com/BunrattyCastleAndFolkPark)

Burncourt Castle

County Tipperary

Internal view of north-east wall.

ALSO KNOWN AS BURNTCOURT, Clogheen Castle or Everard's Castle, this semi-fortified house was built by Sir Richard Everard, first Baronet Everard of Ballyboy, County Tipperary. The Everard family arrived in Ireland when Martin Everard accompanied Prince John (later King of England) on his visit to Ireland in 1185. Successive members of the family spread through Waterford, Wexford, Meath and Tipperary. Sir Richard's father, Sir John Everard, had very substantial lands and effectively owned the town of Fethard in County Tipperary.

Sir John Everard was an accomplished lawyer and was appointed to the Queen's Bench in 1602 by Elizabeth I. He was appointed to the King's Bench in 1603 by James I/VI, and was knighted in 1605. Of the seven judges on the King's Bench, Sir John was the only Catholic. The Penal Laws eventually made his position untenable and led to his resignation in 1607. Then embarking on a political career, he was elected as Speaker by the Catholic Members of Parliament. The Lord Deputy of Ireland, Sir Arthur Chichester, a staunch Protestant and vigorous enforcer of the Penal Laws, however, insisted that his right-hand man, Sir John Davies, would instead be Speaker. In the face-off Everard took the seat, refusing to vacate it until Davies, an extremely fat man, literally sat on top of him. Despite this fiasco, Sir John played an active role in Parliament until 1615. He continuously campaigned for Catholic causes and was held in high regard by the English Crown, receiving the rights to hold several fairs and markets, and engaging in many business transactions with Richard Boyle, first Earl of Cork.

Sir John's second son, Sir Richard, was created a baronet in 1622 by James I/VI. Sir Richard acquired significant lands in Counties Cork, Limerick and Tipperary. In the 1630s he sold various properties in Cork and Limerick, and used the funds to finance the construction of a large, semi-fortified house near Clogheen in Tipperary, which would later become known as Burncourt. During its construction Sir Richard resided at Ballyboy Castle, a small tower house

View through south-east entrance.

Internal view of south-west wing.

that still survives in scant ruins just east of Clogheen village. He received a grant from Charles I in 1639, creating the manor of Everard's Castle and moved into his magnificent new residence in 1641.

Burncourt is one of the largest and was probably the last of the semi-fortified houses to be built in Ireland. It comprises a central two-storey block with basement and a gabled attic, with four three-storey-over-basement corner towers, also with gables, giving the whole building a grand total of twenty-six gables. The main entrance is centrally placed in the west façade. The windows are all mullioned and transomed, and have hood mouldings overhead. Several fireplaces in the building are made of polished limestone and the walls on the west and east façades have external stone corbels that once supported timber defensive galleries.

In 1641, not long after Sir Richard moved into his new castle, the Irish Rebellion broke out. The aggressive colonisation of Ireland by Protestant settlers from England and Scotland had led to ever-increasing grievance amongst the Irish Catholic gentry. The rebels had planned to seize some key towns and strongholds, and then enter into negotiations with Charles I from a position of strength. The rebellion, however, soon turned into full-scale war. Protestant settlers were robbed and evicted from their lands, farms and houses were burnt, and cattle stolen. The violence escalated into widespread killing of settlers and many fled as refugees to England. Reports of wholesale massacres and atrocities spread rapidly through England and Scotland, provoking fears of an international Catholic conspiracy. The English Parliament then voted, in defiance of the king, to raise forces of its own under the Militia Bill and passed the Adventurers Act in March 1642, promising land in Ireland to speculators who financed the raising of troops. In response, the Catholic Irish organised themselves into the Confederate Assembly of Kilkenny, and so followed the eleven-year Confederate War that was brought to a bloody end with Oliver Cromwell's invasion of Ireland in 1649.

Despite being a staunch Catholic like his father, Sir Richard gave protection to the Protestant English tenants whom he had planted on his estate. A number of their houses had been burnt and their cattle stolen. In 1642, he joined the Catholic Confederates in Kilkenny where he was admitted into the close group of twenty-four members who formed the Supreme Council. After the execution of Charles I in 1649, Sir Richard was listed as one of the twelve commissioners into whose hands the entire control of military and civil affairs of the kingdom was entrusted.

Cromwell arrived in Ireland in 1649 and after the conquest of the south-east, he marched from Youghal to Tipperary in the early days of 1650. On 31 January, he recorded in his dispatch to the English Parliament, 'I marched to a strong house, called Clogheen, belonging to Sir Richard Everard, who is one of the Supreme Council.' As the Cromwellian army approached, Sir Richard's wife, Lady Catherine, set fire to the castle, intent on making it of little use to the Cromwellians, before fleeing the area. Local tradition relates that the castle was seven years in building, seven years lived in and seven days burning.

Sir Richard fell back to Limerick, where he defended the city against Cromwell's army. After five months of heavy fighting and the surrender of the city, he was refused pardon, along with twenty-three other men, and hanged by Cromwell's son-in-law, General Henry Ireton.

The Civil Survey of 1654, refers to 'Sir Richard Everards Mansion house, called Everards Castle the walls only standinge and some cabbins within a bawne, the said house beinge burned is yett without repaire'. The burnt-out castle soon became known as Burncourt and was thereafter abandoned.

Burncourt is in the ownership of the Irish State under the OPW. It is located on private property but can be easily viewed from the nearby road.

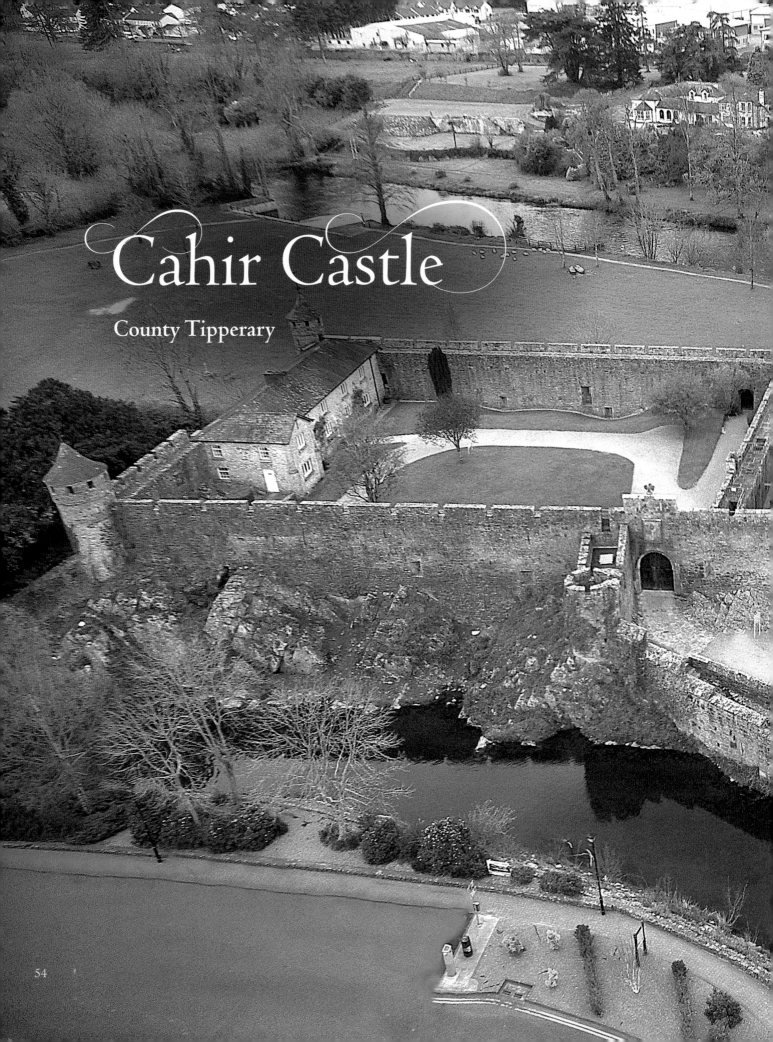

Cahir Castle

County Tipperary

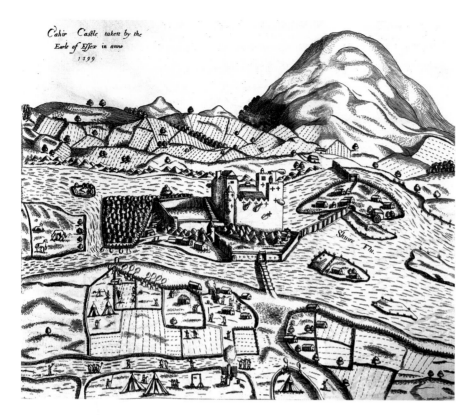

Cahir Castle taken by the Earle of Essex in anno 1599

CAHIR CASTLE AND THE TOWN that surrounds it derive their name from the Irish '*cathair*', meaning 'stone ring fort'. The Book of Lecan, a medieval Irish manuscript, describes the destruction of such a ring fort here in the third century and it is likely that, over the centuries, a series of forts was constructed on, or near, the site of the present castle.

In 1215, the barony of Cahir was granted to Philip of Worcester and it was either he or his nephew and heir, William, who began building Cahir Castle. The main tower, hall and sections of the inner ward all date from this period. At this time the main tower had an entrance gateway in the south wall, which controlled access into the inner ward. The hall, built along the west wall of the ward, was a space for formal meetings of the manor court as well as for feasting. The castle passed to the de Bermingham family with the marriage of William's daughter, Basilia, to Milo de Bermingham. Following the arrest, escape and subsequent execution of William Bermingham in 1332, the Cahir lands were forfeited to the Crown.

In 1375, the manor of Cahir was granted to James Butler, third Earl of Ormond, as a reward for his loyalty to Edward III. His son, James '*Gallda*' or 'the Foreigner', the product of a well-publicised illicit affair with his niece, based himself at Cahir, greatly expanding the castle and establishing the Cahir branch of the Butler family. In 1542, Thomas Butler was created Baron Cahir by Henry VIII. The Barons of Cahir occupied a vulnerable position between the borders of two powerful rivals, the Earls of Ormond and the Earls of Desmond. Every opportunity was taken to strengthen the castle and make it highly defensible, so that by the end of the sixteenth century it was considered the strongest fortress in all Ireland. The curtain walls around the inner ward were raised and extended outwards to accommodate a tower at the north-west corner, the entrance in the main tower was blocked up and a new, much stronger entrance with portcullis created beside a circular tower just to the east. A large rectangular enclosure with small round corner towers was built to the south, creating an outer ward.

During the Nine Years' War (1595–1603), Cahir Castle came under the scrutiny of Elizabeth I's military commander for Ireland, Robert Devereux, second Earl of Essex. Essex's secretary described it as 'the only famous castle in Ireland which was thought impregnable and is the bulwark for Munster, and a safe retreat for all the agents of Spain and Rome'. In May 1599, Essex marched on the castle with nearly 18,000 troops, the largest army ever seen in Ireland. At the time, the castle belonged to Thomas Butler, fourth Baron Cahir, but it was in the custody of his brother, James. Lord Cahir assured Essex that his brother would surrender the castle; however, he did not submit.

On Sunday 27 May, Essex opened fire with a cannon placed close to the castle wall at point-blank range. On the second shot the cannon's carriage broke and then took a day and a half to repair. On the third shot, the cannonball stuck in the barrel, creating a further delay. When it was eventually released a relentless rain of shots pounded the castle and by the evening the east wall had been breached. During the night James and his garrison attempted to sneak away but were spotted by the English army. At least eighty of the castle garrison were killed but James and a few men managed to dive into the river, escaping under a watermill. Essex made much of the castle's capture but Elizabeth I was not impressed, describing James and the castle garrison as only a rabble of rogues. Essex later came under heavy criticism and his campaign in Ireland deemed an expensive failure. His objective had been to return to England with the rebel leader, Hugh O'Neill, the Earl of Tyrone's head on a stick, but instead he had dallied for months in Munster before making a treaty with O'Neill. He was charged with treason, swiftly convicted and executed in February 1601.

Lord Cahir soon regained the castle and the Butlers continued on in relative peace until the Confederate Wars of the mid-seventeenth century. In 1647, the castle was again threatened with siege, this time by Murrough 'of the Burnings' O'Brien, sixth Baron Inchiquin. Lord Inchiquin obtained his nickname from his ruthless treatment of Irish Catholics who would not convert to Anglicanism, usually by burning their houses, land and crops. With the memory

(L–r): View of the main tower from north; view into the portcullis entrance.

View of hall from inner ward.

View of castle from the town bridge.

of the siege by Essex still in living memory, the castle was swiftly surrendered. A few years later the castle was again under threat, this time by Oliver Cromwell. Cromwell's letter, addressed to the Governor of Cahir Castle, dated 24 February 1649, is preserved in the British Museum:

> Sir, – Having brought the Army and my cannon near this place, – according to my usual manner in summoning places, I thought fit to offer you Terms honourable for soldiers: That you may march away, with your baggage, arms and colours; free from injury or violence. But if I be necessitated to bend my cannon upon you, you must expect the extremity usual in such cases.
>
> To avoid blood, this is offered to you by, your servant,
>
> Oliver Cromwell

Again the castle was surrendered without a shot being fired. The Cahir estate was confiscated but never allotted to the Cromwellians and, following the restoration of Charles II, it was returned to the Butlers in 1622. In 1677, Piers Butler, the sixth Baron Cahir, died 'of a surfeit of claret'. Theobald, the seventh Baron, sat in James II's Irish Parliament in 1689, and was outlawed in 1691, but restored to his honours in 1693. The Butlers of Cahir remained Catholic and continued on discreetly throughout the eighteenth century until James, the ninth Baron, moved to France where he died in 1786. His brother, Piers, became the tenth Baron but died in Paris two years later. The title then passed to the son of the ninth Baron, Richard, who in 1816 was elevated to the titles Viscount Cahir and Earl of Glengall. It was Richard, first Earl of Glengall, who built the Swiss Cottage, about 2km south of the castle, a delightful ornamental cottage designed by the famous Regency architect John Nash.

When Richard's son, also named Richard, became the second Earl of Glengall in 1819, the estate was in a financially perilous position. In 1834, however, he married a wealthy heiress, Margaret Mellish, the daughter of an English army contractor who had owned valuable property in London's docklands. Margaret's initial marriage settlement was £100,000, about €10 million in today's money, and seemingly there was much more to come. She and her new husband soon embarked on an extravagant spending spree.

The earl employed the Clonmel architect William Tinsley, and a programme of improvements to the Cahir estate was established, which included the restoration of Cahir Caste and the rebuilding of much of the town. There are few records of exactly what work was undertaken but the earl recorded in his notebook that 'there are so many inconveniences in the castle for making it a residence that after long consideration I doubt the prudence of doing so. The Castle of Cahir should always be preserved, as the ancient Memorial of the Family.' In these years extensive rebuilding of the castle was undertaken and the two-storey house at the outer ward was also constructed.

Eventually, in 1848, the trustees of his wife's inheritance and her sister, Lady Elizabeth Thynne, put a stop to the spending. That year the second Earl's debts amounted to about £300,000, or about €30 million in today's money. The following year he was declared bankrupt and in 1853 his estates were sold through the Encumbered Estates Court. The second Earl of Glengall was still bankrupt when he died in 1858 and, as he had no male heir, all of his titles became extinct.

His daughter, Lady Margaret Charteris, and her son, Lieutenant Colonel Richard Butler Charteris, regained possession of the castle and lived nearby at Cahir Lodge. The Lieutenant Colonel died in 1961 and in 1964 Cahir Castle was taken into state care as a National Monument. At that time the castle's hall was the only building still in use. Subsequently, extensive conservation and restoration works on the entire castle were undertaken by the state. Today, both the castle and the nearby Swiss Cottage are in the care of the OPW and open to the public daily.

Castle Oliver

County Limerick

A 1836 engraving of Isabella (left) and Elizabeth Oliver Gascoigne by J. Thomson.

Tʜᴇ ғɪʀsᴛ ᴄᴀsᴛʟᴇ ᴏɴ ᴛʜɪs sɪᴛᴇ was named Clonodfoy, deriving its name from the Irish '*cloch an Otbhaidhigh*', meaning 'the stone structure of Otway'. The Anglo-Norman Otway family settled here at the end of the twelfth century. The Clonodfoy lands passed through the hands of the Roches and then to the Fitzharris family, who acquired ownership at the end of the sixteenth century. In the Civil Survey of 1654, Sir Edward Fitzharris is described as owning 'an old ruined house, a bawn, a stable, an orchard and garden thereupon'. Fitzharris was a Catholic and a staunch supporter of King Charles I and subsequently found himself transported 'to Hell or to Connaught' during Cromwell's conquest of Ireland.

The Clonodfoy estate was then granted to one of Cromwell's soldiers of fortune, Ambrose Jones, who in turn sold it to another of Cromwell's soldiers, Captain Robert Oliver. Oliver had also received large grants of land in County Limerick. He promptly renamed Clonodfoy Castle Oliver, and set about starting the foundations of a substantial dynasty. By the time of the death in 1798 of his great-great-grandson, the Right Hon. Silver Oliver, the family was in control of a vast estate of over 20,000 acres in County Limerick as well as other lands in Counties Cork and Kerry, including numerous farms, cottages, mills and hamlets. Robert's second son, Charles Silver Oliver, was left in control and based himself at Inchera, in County Cork, where he married Elizabeth Morris, and slyly kept his mistress, Mary Green, at Castle Oliver.

Mary Green bore him at least four illegitimate children, all of whom took the surname Oliver. In 1818, the youngest, Eliza, met Ensign Edward Gilbert, who was stationed in Cork, when she was just fourteen. She married him two years later and shortly after her seventeenth birthday gave birth to Elizabeth Rosanna Gilbert. Elizabeth became a Spanish dancer and performer and a notorious manipulator of men. Known as Lola Montez, she worked her way through London, Germany and Poland before becoming a favourite of Tsar Nicholas I in Russia. When she met King Ludwig of Bavaria he soon made her his mistress. The Jesuits in Munich described her as 'an emissary of Satan … an apocalyptic whore'. Later, passing through London and Australia, with several affairs and short marriages, she went to America where she appeared on the stages of Broadway with a horse whip with which she kept unruly members of the audience in check. She died of pneumonia at forty-two and is buried in Greenwood cemetery in Brooklyn, New York.

Charles Silver Oliver was a ruthless and much hated landlord. A monument erected in the nearby village of Kilfinane records one of his wicked deeds when, without trial, he hanged, drew and quartered a popular local United Irishman, Patrick 'Staker' Wallis, and placed his head on a stake on the top of Kilfinane market hall. In his later years Charles moved to London, leaving his steward, another tyrant, James Galloway, in charge of Castle Oliver. Under Galloway's care, the castle was allowed to fall into such a state or disrepair that it became fit only for demolition. Galloway apparently refused to leave the castle even on death and it is said that his ghost still haunts the surrounding woods and pathways.

Charles's brother, Richard Philip Oliver, eventually inherited Castle Oliver, but lived in England at Parlington Hall in Yorkshire. He and his wife, Mary, had inherited Parlington from Sir Thomas Gascoigne in 1810. As a condition to this inheritance he had taken the additional name Gascoigne, becoming Richard Philip Oliver Gascoigne. The Parlington Hall estate amounted to 6,000 acres of land and included several very profitable coal mines that brought in the vast annual income of £12,000 (about €13 million in today's money). Richard and Mary had two sons (Thomas, born in 1806, and Richard (junior), born in 1808) and two daughters (Isabella, born in 1810, and Elizabeth, born in 1812). Their mother, Mary, died in 1815, both Thomas and Richard (junior) died in 1842, and their father in 1843,

View of the castle from the south.

leaving Isabella and Elizabeth as heirs to a vast fortune that included the estates of Parlington and another English stately home, Lotherton Hall, as well as Castle Oliver and a number of other Irish properties.

At this time Isabella was thirty-three years old and Elizabeth thirty-one, and unusually for the period, both were still unmarried. They were also active artisans with Isabella's interest in woodturning the subject of a book she published in 1842 under a male pseudonym.

Following the death of their father they engaged on a frenzy of philanthropic spending, building schools, churches and almshouses. In 1844, the sisters visited their Irish estates and, seeing the neglect of the old castle and estate, and also the misery that the Great Famine was bringing to the local population, decided on building a new castle, in an attempt to bring employment and prosperity to the area.

Choosing the Scottish Baronial style, they employed the architect George Fowler Jones, who had worked for the sisters on other projects. The plans are signed and dated by Jones on 24 June 1845. Jones named his first child Gascoigne, after the sisters, and his monogram is inscribed on the gable end of the castle. Between 1846 and 1850, £14,000, or about €10 million in today's money, was channelled into the castle's construction with the immaculately cut and dressed red sandstone being quarried on the estate, near Kilfinane. According to names and dates found high on the ceilings, Isabella and Elizabeth were still finishing the interior twelve years later, designing and executing both the stained-glass work and verre églomisé (back-painted glass panels), which ornamented the ballroom fireplace.

As well as an architect, George Fowler Jones was also a keen photographer in the very earliest days of the medium. He became a pupil to William Fox Talbot, inventor of the negative/positive process and his photographs of Castle Oliver represent some of the earliest-known photographs of stately homes in Ireland.

Castle Oliver has a huge tower-like keep, many stepped gables and corbelled oriels. A terrace with a pierced parapet featuring heraldic beasts runs along the two principal sides of the castle. The framework of the high pitched roof was

View of the large drawing room.

One of the castle bedrooms.

EXPLORING IRELAND'S CASTLES

made of iron and is considered very much ahead of its time. Underneath its grand reception rooms, the castle wine cellar was the largest in Ireland, able to accommodate tens of thousands of bottles.

During their time in Ireland, both the Gascoigne sisters found husbands. In 1850, Isabella married Captain Frederick Charles Trench and in 1852, Elizabeth married her brother-in-law's cousin, Captain Frederick Mason Trench, the second Baron Ashtown. Lord Ashtown already had two sons and two daughters from his previous marriage. As an indication of the copious consumption that took place during Elizabeth's wedding, a list of wines sent from Parlington Hall to Castle Oliver included 231 dozen bottles of port, madeira and claret and 105 half-dozen others, a total of more than 3,400 bottles. Elizabeth's dowry paid for Lord Ashtown's family seat, Woodlawn House in County Galway, to be lavishly extended to become one of the finest country houses in the county.

Isabella and her husband later returned to Parlington Hall. Their only child, Richard Frederick Thomas Trench Gascoigne, born in 1851, inherited Parlington on Isabella's death in 1891.

Elizabeth, now Lady Ashtown, died childless on 23 February 1893, at the age of eighty-one, having survived her husband by thirteen years. In the latter years of her life she moved to the Hotel National, in Montreux, Switzerland, a favoured destination of the wealthy aristocracy, leaving Castle Oliver in the hands of her husband's grandson, the Hon. William Cosby Trench. The two Gascoigne sisters were born two years apart, both married men named Frederick Trench two years apart, and died two years apart.

Much of Castle Oliver's lands were sold through the Land Acts of the early 1900s, and in 1924 the elderly wheelchair-bound William decided to sell up entirely. On 8 April 1924, 900 lots were offered for auction, being 'the contents of all principal ground and first floor rooms, plus a fourth day's sale being the contents of 8 bedrooms on the top floor and of 6 servants bedrooms, also contents of kitchen and a large quantity of sundry effects to be sold in the yard'. The castle itself, however, failed to find a buyer.

William's two sons, Walter and Algernon, spent much of their life in Kenya, and visited Castle Oliver only occasionally. When William died in 1944, Walter returned to Ireland with the intention of selling the castle, but instead tried to resurrect its farm. Walter's daughter, Norah, described the conditions inside the castle in 1953 as: 'just an empty castle with very little furniture, no electricity and no telephone. We were virtually squatting – very uncomfortable beds, lanterns to see by and a bathroom miles away down the back passage beyond the circular stairs'.

After the death of his first wife, Walter married Gwendoline (Lynn) Turner, but died of a sudden heart attack whilst attending a pig symposium in Bagenalstown, County Carlow, only six weeks after their wedding. Walter's daughters had no interest in running the castle and it was sold to a Danish businessman named Gad, with the condition that Lynn stay on to manage the castle farm as he would spend only half his time there. Gad replaced large sections of the roof, replaced old leaking windows with teak frames, and in an attempt to derive an income from the castle from letting, updated some of the bedroom suites. Lynn and Gad ended up becoming a couple, but Gad died in Denmark before their wedding. Lynn stayed on at the castle, running the farm successfully until 1978.

Following her departure the remains of the once-mighty estate began to deteriorate rapidly. It changed hands several times and when the bank repossessed the property from a subsequent owner, they broke up the land, farm and lodges into separate lots. The castle again failed to find a buyer, fell further into decay and suffered at the hands of vandals and thieves.

In 2006, Castle Oliver found new owners who restored it to its previous splendour, and operated it as a wedding venue, before selling the castle in 2015. Castle Oliver is now a private family home and is not open to the public.

Charleville Forest Castle

County Offaly

View of the castle from the north-west.

CHARLEVILLE FOREST CASTLE was built by Charles William Bury in the early years of the nineteenth century. It is generally recognised as the earliest, and best, of the neo-Gothic castles in Ireland.

The origins of the Charleville Forest estate lie in a grant of 5,000 acres near Tullamore made to Sir John Moore in 1622. Sir John also inherited considerable land from his father in 1633, bringing his total holding up to nearly 18,000 acres. He leased the estate to his brother-in-law, Sir Robert Forth, for a period of eighty-one years at a rent of £100 per year. Forth built a house here named Redwood, constructed mainly of oak taken from the surrounding forest. The house was later let to a succession of tenants.

In 1715, John Moore was sworn into the Irish Privy Council and raised to the Peerage of Ireland as Baron Moore. In 1758, his son, Charles, was further elevated, becoming Earl of Charleville. Charles died childless in 1764, and Charles William Bury, the grandson of Lord Charleville's sister, found himself the heir to a very considerable fortune, including an estate of 23,000 acres. At the time of his inheritance Bury was just six months old – his father had died in a bathing accident in Dublin just before his birth. The estate was placed in his mother's care until he reached adulthood in 1785. The celebration of his twenty-first birthday did not go without incident. A hot-air balloon had been procured, with an ascent attempted near the town of Tullamore, resulting in the world's first known aviation disaster. The balloon collided with a chimney on the town barracks and caught fire. It then bounced along the rooftops, starting an inferno which consumed more than a hundred houses. Bury distributed £550 amongst the unfortunate townsfolk to alleviate their suffering, in those days a very substantial sum. He later oversaw the rebuilding of the town, which, with the arrival of Grand Canal in 1798, linking it with Dublin, enjoyed considerable prosperity.

Bury's inheritance allowed him to live in opulence. He had a town house in London and he also travelled widely on the Continent. He was MP for Kilmallock between 1791 and 1797, and in 1797 was raised to the Peerage of Ireland as Baron Tullamore. In 1800, he was made Viscount Charleville and received a considerable sum of money from the government, apparently in return (some suggest a bribe) for supporting the Act of Union. Six years later he was created Earl of Charleville, reviving the title of his grandmother's brother. Seeking a family seat befitting his title, he decided on replacing the old Redwood house with a Georgian Gothic villa. A number of drawings held in the Irish Architectural Archive in Dublin are thought to have been drawn by Lord Charleville and he wrote of his intention 'to create a structure exhibiting specimens of Gothic architecture but maintaining convenience and modern refinements in luxury'. Horace Walpole's Gothic marvel, Strawberry Hill, in London, was a major influence.

About 1800, Lord Charleville employed the architect Francis Johnston to build Charleville Forest Castle. Johnston had already proven himself a master of the classical style with Townley Hall in County Louth but had limited experience of Gothic. Sir Charles Coote's 1801 book, *General view of the agriculture and manufactures of the King's County*, records Charleville Forest just as construction was getting under way:

> The fine demesne of Charleville … contains nearly 1500 statute acres, most delightfully wooded with fine full grown timber, and a considerable part is planted with young trees … The materials for a superb mansion are now preparing, and a farmyard is building at a proper distance, with all suitable offices which are stated. A lake of near eighty plantation acres, has been cut out by the present Lord, and is interspersed with islands thickly planted, which afford fine cover to swans, and wild fowl of all kinds, that resort the lake, and breed here … A lesser lake adorns the opposite end of the demesne, and through all the plantations, are elegant drives cut in serpentine forms. The sublime appearance of the Slieve Bloom Mountains, the adjoining castles in ruins, and the internal artificial beauties catch the eye through best disposed vistas, and complete this delightful landscape.

Johnston's first plans for Charleville Forest date from February 1801. Work progressed slowly and it was eight years later that the castle was officially opened for public display.

(L–r): The first-floor saloon; the main stairs, said to be haunted by the third Earl's daughter, Harriet, who fell three floors while attempting to slide down the balustrade.

(L–r): View from first-floor gallery to castle entrance; the drawing room.

The castle is constructed of fine cut stone, brought from the nearby Ballyduff quarry, and comprises a high square battlemented block with corner towers. On the entrance front, the corner tower on the right is octagonal and heavily machicolated, whilst the tower on the left is round, slender and rising to a height of nearly 40 metres. In the centre, the entrance door and the window over it are surmounted by a massive corbelled arch. To the west of the castle runs a long, low range of battlemented offices. The castle interior has been described as the most splendid neo-Gothic interior in Ireland. From the hall a straight flight of steps rises to a set of intricately carved doors, beyond which is a vast saloon or gallery running the whole length of the garden front. Its elaborate, plaster fan-vaulted ceiling appears to defy gravity, and the fireplaces, bookcases and window surrounds all exhibit vivacious Gothic styling. The dining room and drawing room are also of vast proportions. On the same level the octagonal tower contains a library and the round tower a small boudoir with plaster vaulting topped by an eight-pointed star.

The first official dinner party at the castle had a dazzling list of guests, which included Lord and Lady Rosse, Lord and Lady Ashtown, Lady Somerset, Lady Lennox, Sir Charles Vernon and the guests of honour, the Viceroy, the Duke of Richmond, and his wife. As the Viceroy approached, his carriage was met by two bands playing 'God Save the King'. The horses were taken from the carriage and the Tullamore yeomen carefully pulled it up to the castle. Lady Charleville had the servants turned out in full-dress liveries, with the butlers fitted out in a uniform of blue and scarlet.

The party was intended to impress: Lord Charleville hoped the Viceroy would wield his considerable influence in helping him obtain the lucrative position of Irish Postmastership for which he had recently applied. Lord Charleville, unfortunately, failed to secure the position, which caused him considerable distress. Along with the huge expenditure of building the castle, the family were living well beyond their means and heading towards bankruptcy.

When Lord Charleville died in 1835, the estate was financially 'embarrassed', and in 1844, property in Limerick had to be sold off. The castle was then closed up, and the second Earl moved to Berlin where he lived in much reduced circumstances. The castle was opened again in 1851, when the third Earl returned to Ireland, but he died eight years later, leaving the estate and title to his seven-year-old son. In 1861, the third Earl's daughter, Harriet, fell from the main staircase whilst attempting to slide down the balustrade. Hitting the floor three storeys down, she was instantly killed. The fourth Earl celebrated his coming of age in 1873, but died the following year. The fifth and final Earl of Charleville, Alfred Bury, succeeded in 1874, but died childless in 1875, aged forty-six. Within sixty years of the castle's construction it had passed through five members of the Bury family and the title, Earl of Charleville, was now extinguished.

Lady Emily Alfreda Julia Bury, daughter of the third Earl, inherited the castle and employed the architect William Morris to redecorate several rooms. By 1901, the castle was proving impractical and Lady Emily left for the Continent. The 1901 census records the sixty rooms of the castle occupied by just two servants. After her death in Paris in 1931,

The boudoir in the round tower.

the estate passed to her son, Charles Kenneth Howard Bury. In 1948, the contents of Charleville Forest were sold by public auction and it was left empty. In 1962, the castle appeared in the magazine *Country Life*, dazzling the readers with photographs showing the extraordinary scale of the interiors. The photographs, however, had been a set-up, with furniture borrowed from Belvedere House. After the death of Charles in 1964, the estate passed to a cousin, Major William Bacon Hutton, who assumed the additional surname of Bury as part of his inheritance.

The castle was then abandoned. One of the few original interior pieces was a vast painting measuring more than 6 metres in width. Being too large to be removed it was left in the castle where it was vandalised. Twenty-two years later the painting was discovered to be a long-lost masterpiece by the artist Matthew William Peters, painted in 1789. Carefully removed from its frame, the painting was rolled up and carried off the estate on the back of a tractor. It took two years to restore and is now on loan to the Beaverbrook Art Gallery in Canada.

In 1971, Michael McMullen purchased a 35-year lease of the castle from the Hutton Burys, who continued to farm the surrounding 2,000 acres. The castle had not been occupied for decades, every window had been vandalised and the lead stripped from its roof. Enlisting the help of a builder and undertaking much needed restoration work himself, he made the castle weathertight. Thankfully, none of the elaborate plaster ceilings had collapsed. Various disagreements between McMullen and the Hutton Burys followed and several legal actions were taken in the 1970s and 1980s.

The castle changed hands again when Bridget Vance and her parents planned to use it as a hotel and a venue for weddings. They undertook further restoration work and in 1994 transferred ownership into the Charleville Castle Heritage Trust, a voluntary not-for-profit organisation. Today, the castle is managed by Dudley Stewart who leads a team of volunteers who help maintain and restore the castle. Various festivals are held in the grounds to raise funds, including the annual Castlepalooza Music Festival. The castle is open to the public and guided tours are run daily (check with the castle for further details: www.charlevillecastle.ie).

Clonony Castle

County Offaly

BUILT IN THE EARLY 1500s, Clonony Castle was one of several tower houses in the possession of the MacCoughlan family, whose power base was in west Offaly during the sixteenth century.

The tower measures about 11 metres by 8 metres at its base, and rises to a height of about 15 metres. The steps and single-storey arched entrance attached to the western side of the tower were added in the 1800s. Surrounding the tower are the remains of a rectangular bawn measuring about 52 metres by 37 metres, with flanking towers on the west and south corners.

The tower doorway is protected from above by a murder hole, where boiling water, oil or other projectiles could be thrown down on unwelcome visitors. The tower has three storeys, accessed by a spiral staircase in the south-west corner. Typical of spiral stairs in tower houses, it ascends in a clockwise direction, designed to leave the defender's sword-wielding right arm free to drive blows onto any attacking force coming up the stairs from below. The first floor has a stone barrel-vaulted ceiling, protecting the upper storey, which would have contained the lord's living area. There is a garderobe on the north-east angle, where the castle occupants would relieve themselves, and also hang their clothes, so the ammonia would kill any fleas and mites. At roof level there are some remains of a wall walk and a machicolation.

Tradition has it that Clonony Castle was surrendered to Henry VIII by John Óg MacCoughlan and then given to Thomas Boleyn in exchange for the hand in marriage of his daughter Anne. In 1803, some labourers who were quarrying rock for the construction of a barracks nearby made a remarkable discovery in a cave near the base of the castle. In this cave, at a depth of about 2 metres below the surface, they found a large limestone grave slab. Rocks had been piled over the slab to conceal it. Under the slab there was a coffin cut into the solid rock, which contained two skeletons. The slab bore the inscription: 'Here under leys Elisabeth and Mary Bullyn daughters of Thomas Bullyn, Son of George Bullyn, The son of George Bullyn Viscount Rochford, Son of Sir Thomas Bullyn, Erle of Ormond and Willsheere'. The skeletons appeared to be Mary and Elisabeth Bullyn (Boleyn), cousins of the ill-fated Anne Boleyn and second cousins of Queen Elizabeth I.

The full truth has been lost to history; however, it seems likely that the Bullyns (Boleyns) had fled to Ireland to escape the wrath of Henry VIII following his altercation with Anne Boleyn. For her inability to provide the King with an heir, Anne was charged with treasonable adultery with no fewer than five men, as well as with sexual deviation and suspicion of being a witch, for which she was executed in 1536.

Mary and Elisabeth had apparently lived out lonely lives at Clonony, until Elisabeth died from a sudden illness. Mary was devastated at the loss of her sister and ended her own life by throwing herself from the top of the tower. They were buried together, in the same coffin.

Following the discovery of the grave slab, labourers pulled it to the surface, but its immense weight prevented it being moved much more than a few metres from the castle entrance, where it still stands at the base of a hawthorn tree. An article written in 1833 records that following the removal of the slab, an amazing number of centipedes were seen emerging from the cave entrance. About 5 centimetres long and black in colour, they proceeded in their hundreds across a field to a makeshift house where the labourers were living. Here they hung from the roof in clusters like bees after swarming. The labourers' house acquired the name Maggotty House, and after the sudden death of several of its occupants, it was abandoned.

From about 1612, Clonony Castle was occupied by Matthew de Renzi, a German cloth merchant, who had gone bankrupt in London and moved to Ireland to escape his creditors. He seems to have been in constant conflict with the MacCoughlans who were still the most powerful family in the area. Renzi wrote letters to the Lord Deputy in Dublin and King James I in England, describing Sir Seán Óg MacCoughlan, head of the MacCoughlan clan, as 'but a bastard, born in double bastardy'. Seán had ploughed up Renzi's lands and ordered those in the area 'neither to sell to him nor to buy from him, except at excessive rates'. Eventually, Renzi moved to Dublin where he became a government administrator and was knighted in 1627.

Ground-floor chamber.

View to a ground-floor window.

Looking down the spiral staircase
in south-west corner.

First-floor chamber.

From this date Clonony Castle disappears from history until the early nineteenth century, when it comes into the possession of barrister Edmond Molony. Molony set about converting the old castle into a more ornate residence, adding the steps and arched entrance, as well as enlarging many of the castle windows. He put a flagpole on top of the castle battlements, from which he would raise a flag whenever he triumphed at the petty sessions in the local courthouse.

Eventually the castle was abandoned and used only to shelter cows. The vaulted ceiling fell, timber beams and floors rotted away and the stairs between the first and second floors were deliberately destroyed to prevent enthusiastic tourists from accessing the dangerous upper levels.

In 2004, the castle was purchased by the Scottish best-selling author Campbell Armstrong and his American wife, Rebecca. Over the next decade Clonony Castle was restored to its previous splendour. Sadly, Campbell died in 2013.

Rebecca Armstrong opens the castle to the public and gives enthusiastic tours where she tells of fabulous Tudor kings and queens, and the castle's curious connection with the Boleyn sisters.

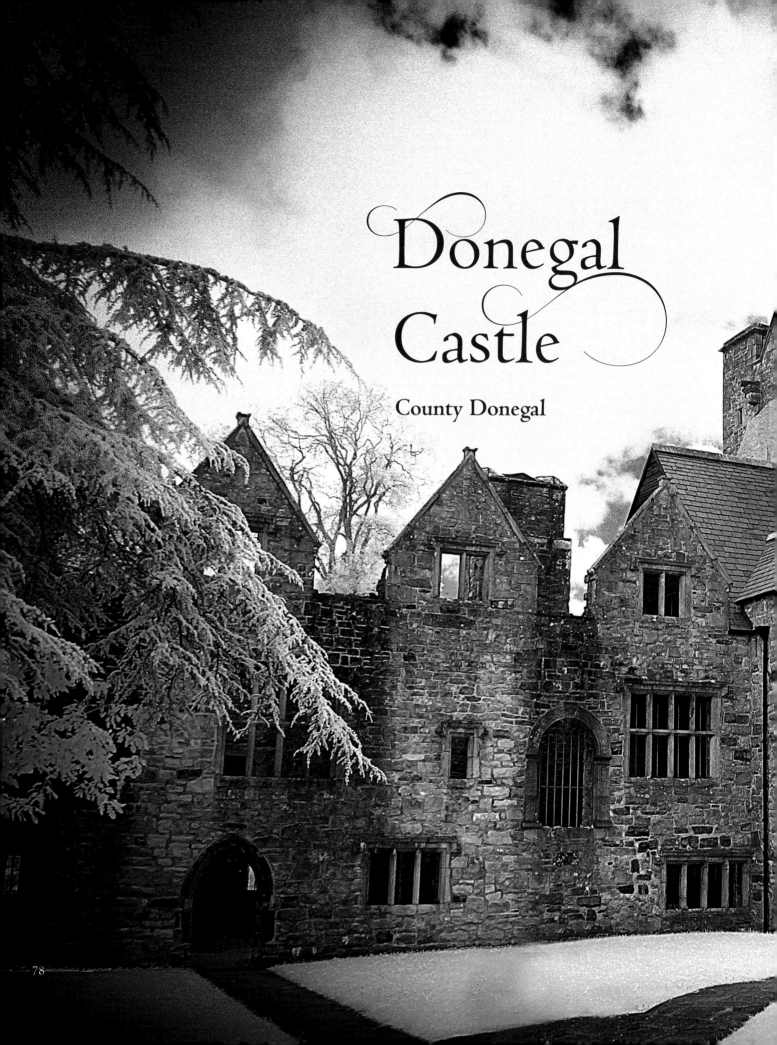

Donegal Castle

County Donegal

View of Basil Brooke's extension wing with original first-floor entrance at centre.

ONEGAL CASTLE BEGAN as a tower house, built by Hugh Roe O'Donnell, leader of the powerful O'Donnell clan. The O'Donnells controlled the district of Tyrconnell that is today called County Donegal. The exact date of the castle's construction is not recorded, though it is assumed to be about 1475, the date that O'Donnell also founded a nearby Franciscan friary. The tower house became the chief residence of the clan and was the scene of many petty domestic feuds and conflict. In 1566, Sir Henry Sidney described the tower house as 'one of the greatest that ever I saw'.

It was deliberately burned in 1589 and partly demolished in 1595, preventing it being garrisoned by English forces, but seems to have been repaired by Hugh Roe O'Donnell, great-grandson of the builder of the original tower house. Hugh went south to fight at the Battle of Kinsale and, after suffering defeat, left Ireland in the Flight of the Earls in 1607, after which the tower house fell into English hands.

In 1610, Basil Brooke was captain of the castle garrison. He had come to Ireland with the English army in 1598, and, after fighting in Munster, was appointed a servitor of the Ulster Plantation and a Commissioner for the settlement of the Church of Ireland. In 1616, he was rewarded for his services with a knighthood and the lease of the castle, and in 1623 received a permanent grant of lands that included the borough of Donegal and the castle.

Sir Basil soon set about transforming the castle into a more comfortable and distinctive residence. Construction seems to have occurred in several stages. The first work carried out was the insertion of the large mullioned and transomed windows into the tower house walls at first- and second-floor levels. Brooke also built unusual projecting turrets, as much ornamental as defensive, on the angles of the south-east wall. Many changes were also made to the castle interior including the addition of several fireplaces. The main fireplace on the first floor of the tower has a magnificent Jacobean chimney piece, elaborately carved with the armorial emblems of Sir Basil and his wife, with swags, scrolls, chains and rosettes.

(L–r): First-floor fireplace with magnificent Jacobean chimney piece; fireplace before restoration, photograph by J. H. Hargrave (c. 1895).

First-floor main chamber.

Second floor with the magnificent
reconstructed oak rafters.

The second phase of construction was the addition of the large T-shaped wing adjoining the tower to the south-west. The wing served two purposes: the addition of a large kitchen on the ground floor and the provision of a new, much grander entrance to the tower house on its first floor. From the ground-floor kitchen of the wing a doorway gave access to the vaulted ground floor of the tower house, which was the main store area of the castle. Timber steps led from the castle courtyard to a decorated doorway in the first floor of the wing. Visitors then entered a hallway with a further flight of timber steps that led to a lobby in the tower house and then on to the main chamber.

Sir Basil's own accommodation was in the tower, where the main chamber on the first floor was used for meetings, dining and entertainment. Above this, on the second floor, were the bedchambers for Sir Basil and his family.

With all his construction, Sir Basil transformed the old O'Donnell castle into a grand Jacobean house. It was still relatively well defended and by retreating into the tower house Sir Basil could comfortably ride out any skirmishes. Access from the ground into the tower was difficult. Wide windows were confined to the first floor and above, and there were loops and holes placed lower in the walls for handguns. The doors between the wing and the tower were also guarded by shot holes in the jambs.

Sir Basil and his son, Sir Henry Brooke, served in turn as Governor of County Donegal. In May 1651, during the Civil War, Sir Henry sided with the Parliamentarians and lost the castle to the Royalist Earl of Clanricarde, but managed to recapture the castle just three days later.

The Brooke family retained the castle for a few more generations but in the eighteenth century it was left to fall into ruin. The castle eventually came into the ownership of the Earl of Arran, who maintained the ruin in good order. In 1898, the Earl donated the castle to the state. The tower house was superbly restored by the OPW in the 1990s with the mansion house left as a well-stabilised ruin.

Donegal Castle is open to the public daily during the summer and on selected days during the winter.

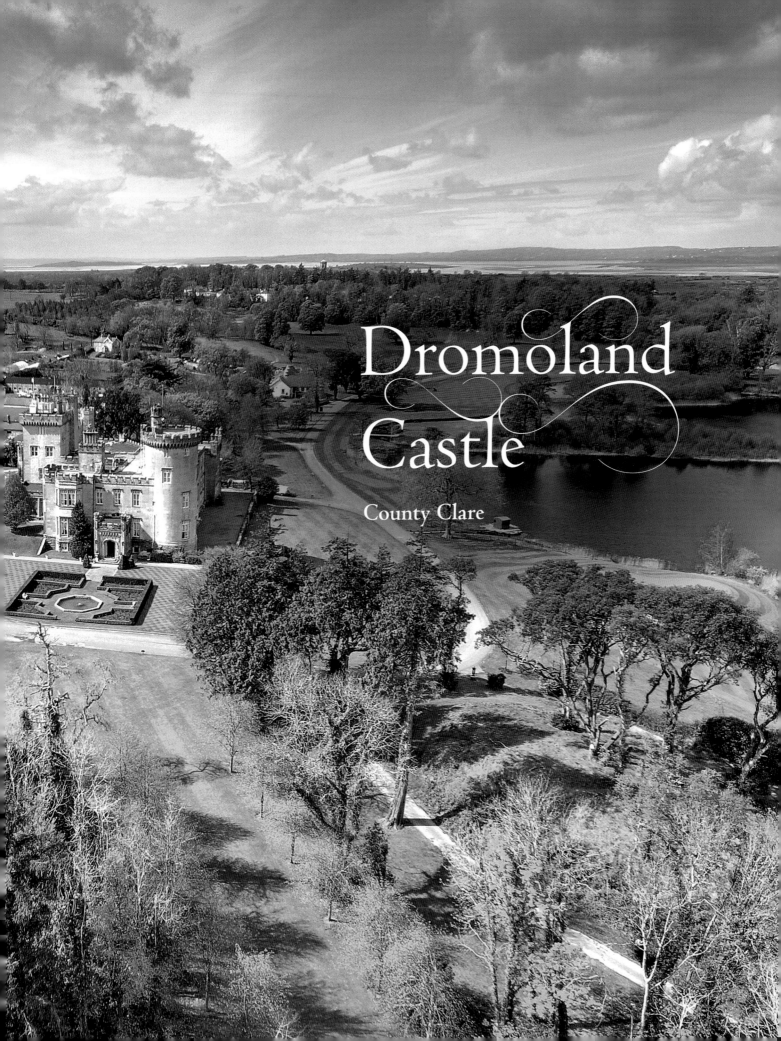

Dromoland
Castle

County Clare

View of castle from south, showing present hotel entrance.

DROMOLAND CASTLE has been home to eight generations of the O'Brien family. The present castle dates from 1835 and is the third structure to be built on the site, the earlier structures being a medieval tower house and an eighteenth-century mansion house.

The Dromoland O'Briens are descended from Brian Boru, High King of Ireland, who died in 1014. After Brian Boru there was a long line of Kings of Thomond until 1542, when Murrough O'Brien surrendered to Henry VIII, pledging his allegiance to the English Crown and converting to Anglicanism. In return for his surrender, Murrough was regranted his lands and created Baron Inchiquin and Earl of Thomond. The Earl of Thomond's chief stronghold was at Bunratty Castle, County Clare (see p. 42). The Dromoland O'Briens were a branch of that family.

The first historical reference to Dromoland occurs when it was listed in Murrough's will, and on his death, in 1551, both Dromoland Castle and Leamaneh Castle were bequeathed to his third son, Donough MacMurrough O'Brien. In 1582, Donough was hanged in Limerick on charges of rebellion and all his property was forfeited to Queen Elizabeth I. Sir George Cusack, the sheriff of County Clare, then took possession of Dromoland. The O'Briens, however, eventually regained the property but it was the subject of various legal disputes and let to William and then Robert Starkey.

In 1684, the freehold of Dromoland was assigned to Sir Donough O'Brien, great-grandson of Donough MacMurrough O'Brien. In 1686, Sir Donough was elevated to the Irish peerage, becoming the first Baronet O'Brien, of Leamaneh and Dromoland. Towards the end of the seventeenth century he relocated his family seat from Leamaneh Castle, on the edge of the Burren in County Clare, to Dromoland. At this time Dromoland was a modest residence comprising a tower house with alterations and additions carried out by the Starkeys. Sir Donough carried out further work on the house and several expenses relating to this are listed in account books. For example, in April 1713, £7 04s was paid to Barnaby Deman for chimney pieces sent to Dromoland, and £12 04s was paid to Mr Gothar the plumber, painter and carver. In September 1713, £6 16s 8d was paid to Samil Cooke for painting the drawing room and buffet. The account books also record payments to masons, carpenters, bricklayers and upholsterers.

Both Sir Donough and his son, Lucius, died in 1717. At this time Lucius's son, Edward, was just twelve years old and Lucius's wife, Catherine (née Keightley), had control of Dromoland until he reached maturity. Catherine planned further alterations and extensions to the house and consulted the architect Thomas Burgh. When Edward reached maturity, becoming the second Baronet, he consulted with architects Thomas Roberts and John Aheron. Various unsigned drawings of the house and plans for landscaping exist from this period, though the exact details of what was built and by whom have been lost to time. Between Sir Donough, the first Baronet, Sir Edward, the second Baronet, and Edward's mother, Catherine, a substantial classical mansion house was built, although it would eventually be totally demolished to make way for the present castle.

Sir Edward was passionate about racehorses and owned Jockey Hall, a house close to the Curragh Racecourse in County Kildare. At Dromoland he renamed the nearby village Newmarket-on-Fergus after the famous thoroughbred horse-racing venue in the town of Newmarket in England. He had an octagonal turret built so that he could observe his horses training around Turret Hill. The turret, designed by John Aheron, was restored in 1998 and is one of the few surviving examples of his work.

In 1788, Daniel Augustus Beaufort described a visit to Dromoland in his *Journey Through County Clare*: 'A large old house not regular and only part of a vast design, intended to connect with a castle, since pulled down, standing between terraces with gravel walks, grassy smooth slopes and distant objects seen through vistas in front. In the rear commanding a small lake, with fine woods overhanging a fine rising ground full of haycocks beyond it. The house covered with jasmine, a great aloe in a tub at the front and many very beautiful trees make this old fashioned place cheerful as well as magnificent.'

In 1812, the second Sir Edward O'Brien, fourth Baronet, began thinking about building a new mansion house at Dromoland. He wrote to his wife, Charlotte, that 'Mr Hopper has given me plans for Dromoland House', but later added 'I think it would be almost as well to build a new house entirely and to content ourselves with the one we have till we can do it to suit our purse and wishes in every respect as we are in no hurry about the matter.' The architect Richard Morrison supplied a design for the house in 1814, and then in 1829, the fourth Baronet approached the brothers James and George Pain, pupils of the great English architect, John Nash, who had recently completed the

View of castle from east, showing original entrance.

Gothic Lough Cutra Castle (see page 158). The Pain brothers produced both classical and Gothic plans for Dromoland, with the Gothic eventually being chosen. The large castle, dominated by a heavily battlemented and machicolated tall round corner tower and square tower, with other towers and a turreted porch, was completed in 1835 and was thought to cost about £56,000, or €6 million in today's money.

The interior of the castle was similar to another of the Pain brothers' castles, Mitchelstown Castle in County Cork (now demolished). A square entrance hall opened into a long single-storey inner hall-like gallery, with the staircase at its far end, and the principal reception rooms running on one side. The rooms at Mitchelstown had elaborate plaster Gothic vaulting whereas those at Dromoland have flat, plain ceilings with simple Gothic cornices. The Keightley Room had many magnificent seventeenth-century portraits that came to Dromoland through the marriage of Lucius, second Baronet, to Catherine Keightley, granddaughter of the Earl of Clarendon and first cousin to both Queen Mary II and Queen Anne.

In 1855, Sir Edward's son, Sir Lucius O'Brien, fifth Baronet, inherited the title of Baron Inchiquin from a distant cousin, the last Marquess of Thomond, becoming the thirteenth Baron Inchiquin.

The land acts of the late nineteenth and early twentieth centuries forced the selling-off of most of the Dromoland estate, thus removing much of Lord Inchiquin's annual income. The once-off payment received in return for the land, however, initially bolstered the family finances and the O'Briens continued living in high style at Dromoland through the remainder of the nineteenth and early twentieth centuries. In 1873, the house staff comprised eighteen servants and in 1911, when the majority of country estates were downsizing, the house staff still comprised fourteen servants: a governess, three nurses, a cook, kitchen maid, three housemaids, a daily maid, schoolroom maid, butler, footman and hall boy. The family retained the privilege given to them by Henry VIII of dressing their servants in a royal livery of scarlet; the O'Brien coat of arms, carved over the castle's entrance porch, bears the same three lions as found on the arms of the English monarchy in the Middle Ages.

In 1902, the fifteenth Baron Inchiquin, Lucius William O'Brien, dismantled the gateway at Leamaneh Castle and re-erected it at the entrance to Dromoland's large walled garden. Little changed inside the castle except for the addition of bathrooms and the installation of electricity. As the twentieth century progressed, the financial position of the Dromoland estate became increasingly stretched. After the death of Lucius, fifteenth Baron Inchiquin, the castle was

North façade of the castle.

Drawing of Dromoland by Reverend F. O. Morris, from his 1880 book, *Picturesque Views of Seats of the Noblemen and Gentlemen of Great Britain and Ireland*.

kept going mainly by the personal wealth of his widow, Lady Ethel Inchiquin. When she died in 1940, her son, Donough Edward Foster O'Brien, sixteenth Baron Inchiquin, returned home, leaving behind a military career and a life in London. He brought his wife, Lady Anne, daughter of Viscount Chelmsford, a Viceroy of India. They maintained Dromoland as a traditional ancestral home for twenty years, first trying to make the estate pay its way as a dairy farm, and then after 1948 by taking in tourists as paying guests.

In 1962, the deteriorating financial position of the estate forced Lord Inchiquin to sell the castle and 350 acres of the surrounding parkland, along with its hunting and fishing rights, to Bernard McDonough, an American industrialist from West Virginia, whose grandparents were born in Ireland. Lord Inchiquin kept 1,000 acres for himself on which he built a new residence, Thomond House. Today Thomond House is home to Conor O'Brien, the present and eighteenth Baron Inchiquin.

McDonough transformed Dromoland Castle from an ancestral home into an opulent hotel. In 1987, the castle was sold to a consortium of mainly Irish American investors and today it operates as a world famous five-star luxury hotel (www.dromoland.ie). In 2017, the castle was renovated and restored at a cost of €20 million. Its famous guests have included George W. Bush, Bill Clinton, Juan Carlos I of Spain, Nelson Mandela, Muhammad Ali, Richard Branson, Jack Nicholson, Johnny Cash, Michael Flatley, Bono and John Travolta.

Dunguaire Castle

County Galway

DUNGUAIRE CASTLE derives its name from the Irish '*Dún Guaire*', meaning 'the Fort of Guaire'. Guaire was the seventh-century King of Connacht who, legend relates, was so generous that his right hand had become longer than his left from constantly giving donations to the poor. One tale tells that his generosity extended even beyond death and when a poor beggar visited the king's grave, his skeletal hand emerged from the ground holding a gold coin.

The medieval Irish manuscript The Book of Lecan praises *Dún Guaire* as 'the fort of lasting fame', and 'the white-sheeted fort of soft stones, habitation of poets and bishops'. King Guaire's hospitality was renowned, though it must have been severely tested by Seanchán Torpéist, the chief bard of Ireland, who visited the castle bringing his 150-strong entourage, along with their servants and dogs. The bard composed the following lines to the king on his departure:

> We depart from thee, O stainless Guaire! We leave with thee our blessing; A year, a quarter, and a month, Have we sojourned with thee, O high-king!
>
> Three times fifty poets, – good and smooth, – Three times fifty students in the poetic art, Each with his servant and dog; They were all fed in the one great house.
>
> Each man had his separate meal; Each man had his separate bed; We never arose at early morning, With contentions without calming.
>
> I declare to thee, O God! Who canst the promise verify, That should we return to our own land, We shall visit thee again, O Guaire, though now we depart.

Even allowing for poetic exaggeration, King Guaire's fortress must have been much larger than the modest sixteenth-century tower house that stands on the site today. It is built on a narrow spit of land, jutting out from the shore of Kinvara Bay. In the shallow waters that surround it rise up several natural springs of fresh water, which originate from a lake at Coole Park about 8 kilometres away. The tower house rises to a height of about 23 metres, with each of its three storeys containing a principal chamber measuring about 7 by 9 metres. Surrounding the tower is an irregular six-sided bawn, with the tower built up against its west wall.

Aerial view from south.

The great hall, laid out for a medieval banquet.

The exact details of its construction have been lost to history, though its builder was probably Eoghan Mantach 'the toothless' O'Heyne, a descendant of King Guaire, and chief of the O'Heyne clan. Eoghan 'the toothless' died in 1588 and was succeeded by his son Aodh Buidhe, 'the yellow', who surrendered the castle to the English Crown and had it regranted to him in 1594.

The castle subsequently came into the hands of the Martin/Martyn family, one of the Tribes of Galway. In 1607, it was held by Oliver Martin and in 1615 he received a grant of rights to hold a Saturday market at Kinvara. In 1642, it was held by Richard Martyn, Mayor of Galway. Richard worked against the Plantation of Connacht in the 1630s, and served on the Supreme Council of the Confederate Catholics in the 1640s. He was a lawyer and in 1631 was admitted to the King's Inn, but was suspended from practice at the Irish Bar in 1635 as a known Catholic. He was permitted to resume practice in 1637 after swearing the Oath of Supremacy.

The Martins later made Tullira, also in County Galway, their principal seat and Dunguaire was let to tenants. Colonel Denis Daly of Raford lived at Dunguaire with his family in 1787 and a garrison was stationed in the castle in 1828. Thereafter, the castle fell into disuse, eventually being reduced to a roofless, windowless shell.

During the early twentieth century the ruined castle was, however, still well cared for by its then owner, Edward Martyn, an Irish playwright and first president of Sinn Féin. Edward employed the caretaker, Mr Hanbury, to watch over the castle before offering it to W. B. Yeats if he would repair it. Yeats, however, had already fixed his interest on Ballylee Castle, north-east of Gort in County Galway, and instead Edward sold Dunguaire to his friend and contemporary, the famous surgeon and literary figure, Oliver St John Gogarty. Gogarty began to repair the castle, though never lived in it. In 1954, the castle was brought by Lady Christabel Ampthill who completed its restoration and made it her permanent home. Lady Ampthill was the infamous ex-wife of John Russell, third Baron Ampthill.

Ground-floor entrance
to spiral staircase.

94

The tower's third floor, used by Lady Ampthill as a guest room.

The couple had never been a good match. Russell, who was exceptionally tall and nicknamed 'Stilts', enjoyed going to fancy-dress balls in drag, whilst his young wife spent her evenings in London with what her husband would refer to as 'detestable young men'.

Trouble erupted in 1921 when Lady Ampthill gave birth to Geoffrey, a miracle son, apparently whilst still being technically a virgin and her husband claiming that their marriage had never been consummated. One explanation was that she had taken a bath immediately after her husband, and used the same sponge. Geoffrey, the fourth Baron Ampthill, never shook off his nickname 'Sponge Baby.' The couple's scandalous 1922 divorce case was the subject of numerous articles in the national and international press.

At Dunguaire, Lady Ampthill was devoted to horse and hound and was the only member of the Galway Blazers hunt still to ride side-saddle. She lived modestly in the castle, employing, Mary, a local woman from Kinvara, as her cook and cleaner. Lady Ampthill added the extension to the castle that became her kitchen; the first floor of the castle was used as her drawing room, the second was her bedroom and the top storey was a room for guests.

Dunguaire Castle was opened to visitors in 1966 and purchased by the Shannon Development Company in 1972. Today it is open to the public between April and mid-October and is a centre for medieval banquets.

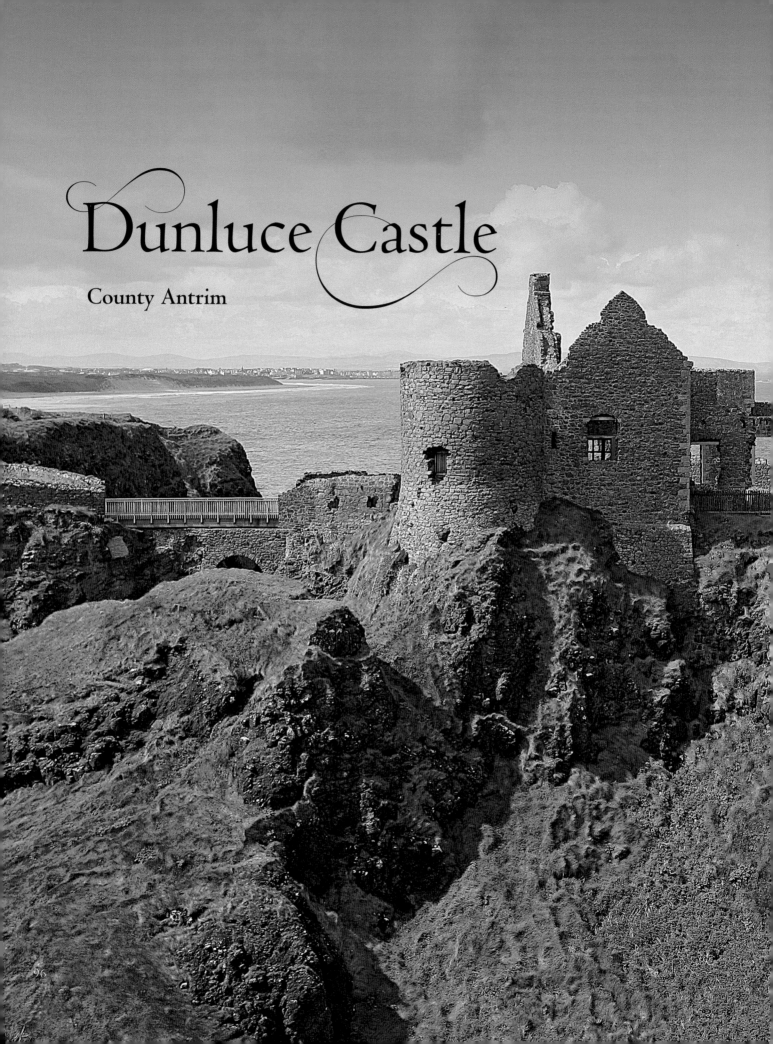

Dunluce Castle

County Antrim

View of Jacobean mansion from north.

FEWER CASTLES CAN BOAST such a striking and romantic site as that of Dunluce. Its dramatic position, perched on the edge of sea cliffs on Antrim's north coast, gives its many visitors fine views of the Scottish Isles to the north-east and the Donegal headlands to the west.

The castle was originally connected to the mainland by a drawbridge, today replaced with a stone archway and a timber bridge. The castle gatehouse was built around 1560 in typical Scottish style with corbelled corner turrets. A strong wall connects the gatehouse with the south-east tower, from where another strong wall formerly connected to the north-east tower. Behind the towers are the remains of a fine Jacobean mansion. Further to the north is the kitchen and buttery and beyond is the castle's inner ward. Below the castle, the whole rock is penetrated by the Mermaid's Cave from where a haunting legend tells of a lost soldier, taken to the deep by a beautiful lady of the sea.

The earliest standing remains of Dunluce Castle date to around 1500 and were built by the MacQuillan clan, the ruling north Antrim family. They controlled an area called 'the Route' which extended between the River Bann and the River Bush. The first definite historical mention of the castle occurred in 1513, when it was transferred from one branch of the MacQuillan family to another. The castle subsequently passed to the MacDonnell family when Evelyn MacQuillan married Colla MacDonnell. Colla died in 1558 and his younger brother, Sorley Boy MacDonnell, then took possession of Dunluce. The MacDonnells, who were descended from the Scottish Clan MacDonald, soon became the dominant force in the area and were almost constantly in conflict with other neighbouring families.

The English Crown became concerned at the growing power of the MacDonnells and in 1584 Queen Elizabeth I sent Sir John Perrott, the Lord Deputy of Ireland, to besiege the castle. He took the castle after a nine-month battle and held it for a short time, plundering Sorley Boy's treasure and taking away, amongst other objects, the Cross of St Columcille, suggesting it would make a fine gift to one of the ladies of the Queen's court 'as a jewel of weight and

Aerial view from north.

bigness'. Sorley Boy regained the castle, when a comrade inside the castle hauled some MacDonnell men up the cliff face in a basket. In 1586, Sorley Boy officially submitted to the Queen and he was made Constable of Dunluce Castle. Peace with the English Crown, however, was not to last.

In 1588, a Spanish Armada ship, the *Girona*, struck nearby Lacada Point. The MacDonnells sheltered some rescued Spanish sailors, sold off much of the ship's recovered cargo, and installed the ship's cannons into the castle gatehouses, all of which aggravated the English. Grievances continued and by the 1590s the Ulster Gaelic chieftains, including the MacDonnells, had risen in rebellion, starting the Nine Years' War. In 1591, Sorley Boy's son Randal became the head of the family following the death of his brother James, and in 1601 he led his men to join Hugh O'Neill at the Battle of Kinsale. The Irish revolt was devastatingly put to an end, but Randal managed to ensure his survival by surrendering to the English at Carrickfergus and was subsequently pardoned. In 1603, King James VI of Scotland ascended the English throne and he granted Randal the territories of the Route and the Glens, giving him control of much of the Antrim coast.

Randal brought across many settlers from Scotland, establishing a town directly outside the walls at Dunluce, and building a series of new settlements and castles across north Antrim, including Kilwaughter (see p. 124), Ballygalley, Glenarm and Ballycastle. By 1620, he had been created Earl of Antrim and his large estates thrived. It was at about this time that the Jacobean mansion was built in the main castle courtyard. In the style of an English manor, it has mullioned windows, tall gables and chimneys and projecting bays.

Randal's son, also called Randal, born in 1609, was brought up at Dunluce in a traditional Gaelic way: Irish was his first language and his father apparently kept a traditional retinue of harpers, bards, priests, mercenaries, kinsmen and bastards around him. In 1625, Randal junior was sent to France, and in 1627 presented at Charles I's court in London. Here he remained for nine years as a guarantor of his father's good behaviour. During this time he became

View of Jacobean mansion from south showing repaired mullioned windows.

wildly extravagant and also acquired a wife, one of the wealthiest people in England, Catherine Manners, the widow of the assassinated Duke of Buckingham.

Catherine retained the use of many of her late husband's properties, as well as owning several of her own. Randal also brought a fine country estate in Hampshire, whilst the couple's main London residence was York House, considered one of the finest and best-appointed mansion houses in Europe. Randal and Catherine's lavish lifestyle, however, eventually got the better of them, and in 1638 they moved to Dunluce in an effort to reduce their expenditure. Randal's father had died two years earlier, and he had succeeded to the title Earl of Antrim. At Dunluce he found himself in control of an estate amounting to nearly 340,000 acres.

Catherine never liked the castle's wild position perched on top of the cliffs and the incessant beating of the waves unnerved her. Her aversion to the place was further provoked in 1639, when, during a dinner party, a section of the kitchen collapsed as some of the cliff face gave way. The dinner, kitchen tables, and all the silverware fell into the stormy sea below. Nine of the kitchen staff fell to their deaths and the kitchen boy only survived by clinging to a corner of the crumbling wall.

Following the outbreak of the Irish Rebellion, Randal was arrested, in 1642, by General Robert Munro, Governor of Carrickfergus. He was imprisoned at Carrickfergus, but escaped and then attempted to negotiate a cessation of hostilities between the English Royalists and Irish Catholic rebels. He was captured again and confined at Carrickfergus, but once again escaped, this time making his way to Kilkenny, the headquarters of the Catholic Confederacy.

His wife, Catherine, now took the opportunity to return to England. The contents of the castle were packed up and sent in a vast shipment to Chester, where they were stored until 1651, when they were seized and sold off by Cromwell's agents. An inventory taken at the time illustrates the exceptionally splendid comfort of the Dunluce household, and includes large crystal-glass mirrors, Persian carpets, chairs upholstered in silk, ebony and ivory cabinets and numerous other items of fine furniture.

During the 1650s, when Cromwell assumed power and deposed the English Crown, Dunluce town and its surrounding lands were granted to Cromwell's soldiers of fortune as payment for their military service during his Irish campaigns. In 1660, Charles II was restored to the throne and five years later Randal regained his estates. Dunluce was occupied for short periods before the MacDonnells moved to Ballymagarry and then Glenarm Castle, which remains their family seat.

Dunluce was abandoned and fell increasingly into decay until 1928, when Randal, the seventh Earl of Antrim, transferred it to the Northern Ireland Government for preservation. Today the castle is managed by Northern Ireland's Department of the Environment and is open to the public daily.

Fiddaun Castle

County Galway

Eight kilometres south-west of Gort in County Galway, Fiddaun Castle is located in an isolated rural setting. It was built on a low, level plane next to Lough Doo and Lough Aslaun, two small lakes that were once joined by water-filled channels, forming a defensive barrier. The castle is unusual in that it is one of the very few tower houses in Ireland with an intact and well-preserved inner bawn.

An outer gatehouse, 165 metres north-east of the castle, controlled access over a drawbridge which crossed one of the water channels. This gatehouse stands three storeys high and has a vaulted lower storey. It is well fortified with loopholes from where the castle garrison had a safe position to fire muskets at any enemy force attempting to access the castle's large 12-acre outer bawn. From the drawbridge an avenue ran through the outer bawn, to a stout gatehouse in the north-west wall of the inner bawn, where a strong iron gate prevented the entry of any foe.

The inner bawn stands over 3.5 metres high and averages about 1.5 metres in thickness. There is a triangular point at the south-west from where men could fire back on anybody attempting to scale the walls. Steps inside the bawn give access to the wall tops where there are many defensive positions. The walls enclose a space measuring about 40 by 25 metres with the tower house at the centre.

The tower itself measures about 12 by 8.5 metres and rises to a height of 24 metres above ground level. It originally contained seven storeys, including the ground floor and attic. The ground floor contains a small guardroom to the right of the entrance, the staircase to the left and a large room measuring about 5.5 by 5 metres in front.

Rising up the stairs to the first floor, here the floor of the main room was carried on beams resting on stone corbels set in the walls. There is another smaller room with a stone floor and a passage leading to a garderobe. Continuing upwards, the main room on the second floor is supported by a stone vault and measures about 6 by 4.5 metres. On the south-east angle is a square, box-shaped bartizan with loopholes. A smaller second-floor chamber had a wooden

View to the tower from the inner bawn.

Tower house entrance.

(L–r): View to the spiral staircase; view down from the fourth floor.

floor supported on beams and led to another square bartizan. Between the two bartizans, muskets could be fired on an enemy approaching or attempting to scale the bawn walls from any direction. Holes in the floors of the bartizans could also be used to fire on an enemy anywhere inside the bawn, thus creating very strong defensive positions.

The third floor rested on beams supported by stone corbels. The main room here measures about 6 by 5 metres and has a fireplace with a well-wrought and moulded stone chimney piece. A secondary room has a small garderobe built into the thickness of one wall. The fourth floor was also supported by beams and corbels and has a main room measuring 5 by 4.5 metres, a smaller room and garderobe. The fifth floor is supported by a stone vault and has a fireplace at the south-west end. The attic floor was carried on corbels and beams, and had steps leading up to the parapet and a watch turret.

Fiddaun Castle was built by Sir Roger O'Shaughnessy, whose father, Sir Dermot, was knighted by Henry VIII in 1545. The O'Shaughnessy were chiefs of the clan of Cineál Aodha, later anglicised to Kinelea, and were in control of the district lying around the town of Gort in County Galway. The clan had three castles, Fiddaun to the west of their territory, Gort to the north and Ardamullivan to the east.

In 1690, Sir Roger O'Shaughnessy and his sixteen-year-old son, William, descendants of the builder of the castle, joined James II's forces at the Battle of the Boyne. They were not wounded, but Sir Roger returned home sick and died in Gort Castle on 11 July 1690, ten days after the battle. In 1697, a decree of formal attainder was brought against both Roger and his son. This meant their act of fighting against William of Orange in the Battle of the Boyne was deemed

Second and third floors (the dividing timber floor is no longer present).

an act of treason, and consequently both men would forfeit their land and civil rights, and were sentenced to death.

The O'Shaughnessy property was seized and later granted to Sir Thomas Prendergast in return for loyal service to King William. Roger's son, Sir William O'Shaughnessy, the last of the O'Shaughnessy chiefs, fled to France. There he pursued a brilliant military career in the French service, becoming a *Maréchal de camp* (Field Marshal) in 1734. He was knighted by the Pope and died whilst still in exile in 1744. Sir Roger's wife, Lady Helena, remained in Ireland where, after the death of her first husband, she married Captain Hugh O'Kelly. She was the last resident of Fiddaun Castle, where she died in 1729.

In 1902, William de Blaquiere, then the proprietor of the castle, transferred its ownership to the Irish state and it was placed in the care of the Board of Works. Substantial restoration and stabilisation followed and today the castle remains a well-preserved ruin.

Fiddaun Castle is in the care of the OPW. To access the castle it is necessary to walk approximately 1 kilometre across private farmland. Permission for this and the key for the castle can be obtained from the nearby Fiddaun House.

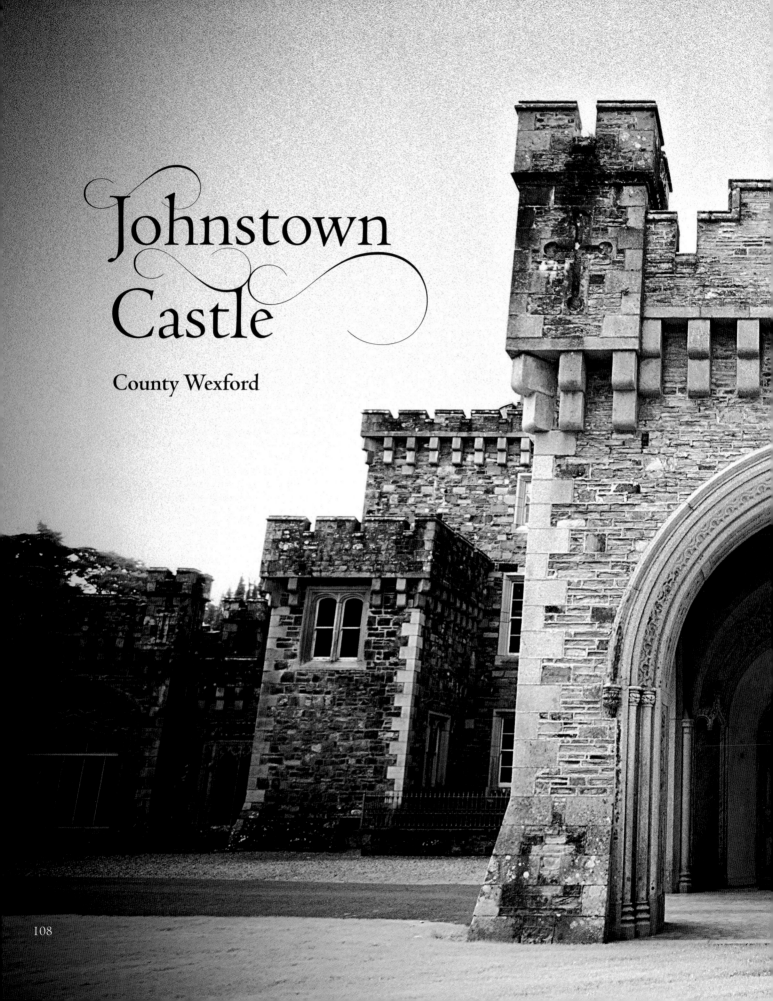

Johnstown Castle

County Wexford

In 1169, Sir Geoffrey de Estemonte was among the thirty knights who landed as part of the advance force of the Anglo-Norman invasion of Ireland. Sir Geoffrey built a motte-and-bailey castle, settling the de Estemonte (Esmonde/Esmond) family in Ireland. Sir Maurice de Estemonte replaced the motte and bailey with a stone castle and his descendant, John Esmonde, later moved the family seat close to the present-day village of Murrintown, County Wexford, where he built a new tower house called Johnstown Castle. Another family member built a second tower house about a kilometre south-west of Johnstown at Rathlannon and in 1608 a list of thirty-eight gentlemen of the barony of Forth records Robert Esmonde at Johnstown and John Esmonde at Rathlannon.

The Esmondes joined the rebellion of 1641 and subsequently had their estates seized in the Cromwellian land confiscations, and were transplanted to Connacht. The Johnstown estate was granted to a Cromwellian soldier, Colonel John Overstreet, and then came by marriage into the possession of the Grogan family. Over subsequent years, the Grogans added a second tower house of similar dimensions to the Esmonde tower, then linked the two towers with a three-storey, five-bay building, transforming the towers into a fine castellated mansion.

By the end of the eighteenth century, the Grogans had become the largest untitled landowners in Ireland, with estates amounting to nearly 20,000 acres. Cornelius Grogan, who was High Sheriff of Wexford and MP for Enniscorthy in the Irish Parliament, became a leader of the rebels in 1798, and as a result was hanged and beheaded on Wexford Bridge. His estate was confiscated; however, his brother, John Knox Grogan, who had fought on the British side, regained ownership after paying a heavy fine in 1802.

John began planning substantial changes to the castle, adding a new three-storey-over-basement block to the south and east sides of the existing castle, then adding great flanking cylindrical towers. John died in 1816 and it was left to his son, Hamilton Knox Grogan, to complete the work. In 1828, Hamilton assumed the additional surname of Morgan, becoming Hamilton Knox Grogan Morgan. This was as a condition to him inheriting a large estate from his father's cousin, Samuel Morgan. The building and remodelling at Johnstown now accelerated and the prolific architect

Aerial view from south.

(Clockwise from top left): Entrance hall or 'Apostles Hall'; dining room; the grand drawing room in 2016; photograph of the grand drawing room (*c.* 1860). The mirrors on the far wall, manufactured in London, were thought to be the largest in Ireland at that time. (*Courtesy of the Irish Agricultural Museum*)

Daniel Robertson, who is well known for his many neo-Gothic mansions, was employed, along with an assistant local architect and builder, Martin Day.

Hamilton was an enthusiastic amateur chemist and one of the additions, connected by a gallery to the east of the castle, was a science laboratory. This was later converted to ballroom, billiard room and a music room. He married a local woman, Sophia Maria Rowe, a patron of the arts and crafts, who employed many skilled artisans, including the woodcarvers Mooney and Sinnott, and an Italian gilder named Barnascone. Thomas Lacy recorded a visit to Johnstown in his 1852 book, *Home Sketches on Both Sides of the Channel*. His description of the castle records its rich ornamentation, interior decoration and landscape design, and runs to several pages. He writes the following about the castle's entrance:

> The approach from the porte cochere to the entrance-hall is by a handsome corridor, with beautiful groined arches, which spring from bosses of the richest character and are equally beautiful in execution and design. The edges of the groinings are of oak, enriched, in some parts, with fine gilding. Curtains of Utrecht velvet of the finest crimson, deeply trimmed and fringed with gold, ornament the splendid Gothic windows on each side of this corridor. The floor of this approach is covered and ornamented with the newest and rarest material which can be applied to such a purpose. The entrance-hall has

Entrance corridor from
the porte-cochère.

a fine appearance; the oak panelling and carving are of the most costly description; amongst other beautiful specimens of carving, both by the hand and by machinery, are the Apostles and the family coat of arms. Nothing can be more truthful and natural than the apostolic figures; the folds of the drapery will enable the most incompetent person to form a judgment of their merit. The skin of a magnificent Bengal tiger, the head finely developed, is spread out as a hearthrug before the fireplace in this hall.

Hamilton's construction projects at the castle also included the building of a large quadrangle stable block, which now houses the wonderful Irish Agricultural Museum, and considerable development of the castle demesne, which stretched to nearly 1,000 acres. The demesne was divided in two with a 220-acre deer park to the north and the remaining pleasure grounds and home farm to the south.

Hamilton's architect, Daniel Robertson, was particularly noted as a landscape designer and his work at Johnstown saw the building of terraces, a sunken garden and three man-made lakes. The Castle Lake covers nearly five acres, is surrounded by two folly towers, and originally had a number of small islands. The Garden Lake covered over two acres and the Lower Lake nearly twelve acres, making it the largest freshwater lake in Wexford and its surrounding counties. The pleasure grounds also included walled gardens, surrounded by three-metre high brick walls. There was a two-acre flower garden, a similarly sized fruit and vegetable garden, as well as a pinery, a one-acre melon garden, a conservatory and two graperies. The gardens were maintained by eighteen staff under the supervision of a head gardener.

Hamilton died in 1854, at the age of forty-six, leaving his estate to be divided between his daughters, but stipulating that the castle would remain the seat and property of his widow, Sophia, for her life. In 1856, Sophia remarried. Her new husband was Sir Thomas Esmonde, a descendant of the Esmondes who built the original castle, and together they continued the various landscaping and construction works. Hamilton's third daughter, Jane, married George Forbes, the seventh Earl of Granard, and they also moved into the castle, necessitating the building of a nursery wing on the western side of the castle. The Granard coat of arms is carved over the porte-cochère and also onto the mantle in the dining room.

Johnstown eventually passed to Lord and Lady Granard's eldest daughter, Adelaide, who married Lord Maurice FitzGerald, son of the Duke of Leinster. After Lord Maurice FitzGerald's death in 1901, Johnstown was managed by his widow and her cousin Captain Ronald Forbes. Lady Adelaide's only son, Captain Gerald Hugh Fitzgerald, was killed in the First World War, and after his mother's death in 1942, the estate passed to his widow, Dorothy Violet Jefferies, and Lady Adelaide's grandson, Maurice Victor Lakin.

In 1945, Johnstown Castle and estate were given as a gift by Dorothy and Maurice to the Irish nation, with provisions that they were to be used solely as an agricultural college and that the ornamental nature of the gardens and grounds would not be altered. The state paid some small outstanding debts on the estate as well as the death duties of Lady Adelaide Jane Frances Fitzgerald and her son, Gerald Hugh Fitzgerald.

Johnstown duly became an agricultural college and over subsequent years the original Esmonde tower was removed and various other changes made. The castle roof was replaced and the main staircase removed and replaced with concrete staircases because of dry rot. The castle was subsequently used as offices for Teagasc, the Agriculture and Food Development Authority, but its condition began to deteriorate and it fell into disuse. Teagasc continues to operate from the Johnstown estate with various offices, laboratories and over 600 acres used for farming research.

The castle interior is currently not accessible; however, the Irish Agricultural Museum, located in the castle stable block, and all the castle grounds and gardens are open to the public daily. A proposed redevelopment of the castle has been officially launched and it is hoped that its interior will also soon be open to the public.

Kanturk Castle

County Cork

View of castle from west.

Dᴇʀᴍᴏᴛ Mᴀᴄᴏ̨ᴡᴇɴ MᴀᴄCᴀʀᴛʜʏ, Lord of Duhallow, began building Kanturk Castle at the end of the sixteenth century, a time when the Nine Years' War had spread from Ulster to all parts of Ireland and 18,000 English soldiers were attempting to assert the Queen's authority. Dermot was one of the signatories on a letter to Pope Clement VIII condemning the Queen's government as worse than that of the pharaohs; George Carew, Lord President of Munster, described him as 'a man for wit and courage nothing inferior to any of the Munster rebels'.

By the middle of 1601, the English had more or less defeated the rebellion in Munster and that year Dermot declared his loyalty to the Queen. His honesty was, however, always doubted and it was only a month later that the Spanish landed at Kinsale and Dermot marched with 500 men to join them. After the Irish defeat at Kinsale, Dermot was taken prisoner, but was pardoned in 1604, and in 1615 was awarded a grant, returning his territory of Duhallow, including Kanturk, by Letters Patent.

The map of Ireland made by John Norden between 1609 and 1611 shows the castle at Cantork (Kanturk). It is a rectangular fortified house, comprising a four-storey rectangular block measuring about 28 metres long by 11 metres wide, flanked at each corner by square five-storey towers, reaching a height of 28 metres. The castle is constructed of rubble limestone from a quarry which lies just north of the castle on the Brogeen River. Other limestone, from a different quarry, was hewn and dressed to be used in the mullioned and transomed windows, the hood mouldings, cornices, quoins, corbel stones, door surrounds and fireplaces.

The main entrance, of Jacobean design, is located on the first floor of the west wall and was probably originally approached from an external flight of timber steps. Directly beneath is a ruined doorway and on the opposite wall a second ground-floor entrance. The interior of the castle had wooden floors throughout as marked by opposing lines of joist sockets. All floors were lit by symmetrically arranged windows. The castle contains numerous fireplaces, in the main block, positioned at the ends of the side walls, and also on most floors of the corner towers. The north-east tower contained wooden stairs with a landing at each corner.

Kanturk Castle was defended by a series of splayed gun loops on the ground floor, located on both faces of the south-east and north-east towers and on the east faces of the south-west and north-west towers. The lack of gun loops on the west side suggests that the castle was protected by a defensive bawn on that side.

One legend relates that a team of seven stonemasons, all named Shane or John, were employed in the castle's construction. Hence it was known as Carrig-na-Shane-saor, or 'the rock of John the Mason'. Another legend tells that the labourers were driven so hard that some dropped dead from exhaustion, their blood being then used to bind the castle's mortar.

Dermot's stepbrother, McAuliffe, who was apparently gifted with second sight, said of the castle that ''Tis too good for the crows to live in, and it will never be finished'. The castle was built as a defence against the English and as news of its massive fortification reached the Privy Council, orders were issued that all construction should cease. Whether the castle was ever completed remains an open question.

In 1632, the castle was mortgaged to Sir Philip Percival. Following the MacCarthy involvement in the 1641 Rebellion, it passed directly into the hands of Percival, whose descendants were later created Earls of Egmont. They held the castle until 1900, when the Countess of Egmont gifted the castle to the National Trust on condition that the building be maintained in the condition in which it was received.

In 1951 the National Trust gave a 1,000-year lease of the castle to An Taisce for the rent of one shilling per year, but also gave £500 annually for its upkeep. It was later placed in the care of the OPW and in 1998 its title deeds transferred to An Taisce, in trust for the people of Ireland. Today it is freely open to the public.

(L–r): View upwards in south corner tower; west wall with magnificent Jacobean first-floor entrance.

Kilkenny Castle

County Kilkenny

Following the Anglo-Norman invasion of Ireland, a motte-and-bailey castle was established at Kilkenny around 1170, by Richard de Clare, Earl of Pembroke, better known as Strongbow. He was succeeded by his son-in-law, Sir William Marshal, who, at the age of forty-three, married Strongbow's seventeen-year-old heiress daughter, Isabel. Marshal was one of the richest men of his day and is described as the greatest knight ever. His long and illustrious career had begun with eking out a living fighting in jousting tournaments and ended up with him as Regent of England and governing the country on behalf of the boy-king Henry III. Much of Marshal's life was spent in England; however, after falling out with King John, he spent the years between 1207 and 1212 in Ireland where he established his lordship of Leinster and built the first stone castle at Kilkenny.

The design Marshal chose resembles the two royal castles built at the same time, under the command of King John: Dublin Castle, begun in 1204, and Limerick Castle (see p. 130), begun in 1211. Each of the castles was intended to comprise a rectangular area enclosed by high walls with a round tower on each corner, and a twin-towered gatehouse near the midpoint of one side. Marshal's great fortress at Kilkenny imposed its plan on all later building, and today, though much changed, the form of three of the original corner towers still survives.

When Marshal died in 1219, he was succeeded in turn by each of his five sons, William, Richard, Gilbert, Walter and Anselm, who all died without male heirs. When Anselm died in 1245, the extensive family properties in England, Wales and Ireland were divided amongst his five sisters and their descendants. County Kilkenny was given to Isabell, the widow of Gilbert de Clare, fifth Earl of Gloucester.

In 1307, the earliest historical description of the castle records it as containing 'a hall, four towers, a chapel, a moat and many other houses necessary to the castle'. The de Clares held Kilkenny until 1314, when Gilbert, the eighth Earl of Gloucester, was killed at the Battle of Bannockburn in Scotland, and his estates were divided amongst his three sisters. Eleanor received the town of Kilkenny, including the castle. She was married to Hugh le Despenser. The Despensers never resided in Ireland and, in 1391, sold Kilkenny Castle to James Butler, the third Earl of Ormond.

The Butlers' origins began with Theobald FitzWalter, an English nobleman, who came with young Prince John to Ireland in 1185. Theobald was granted a large estate and appointed as Chief Butler of Ireland, meaning he had to

Aerial view from the north-west.

(L–r): Carved stone head outside the medieval room; dining room.

ensure there was always sufficient food and drink ready for any king's visit. Under the Prisage of Wine, Theobald, and his descendants were entitled to a levy worth about 15 per cent of all the wine imported into Ireland, which amounted to a very considerable income.

From the early thirteenth century the FitzWalters were known as 'Butlers'. In 1327, James Butler, the eighth generation of Butlers, married Eleanor, a niece of King Edward III, and the following year the King made him Earl of Ormond. It was James's grandson, another James, who bought Kilkenny Castle from the Despensers in 1391. Under the Butlers, Kilkenny flourished throughout the fifteenth and sixteenth centuries, becoming second in importance only to Dublin.

On the outbreak of the Irish Uprising in 1641, James FitzThomas Butler, twelfth Earl of Ormond, fled to Dublin while his Kilkenny estates were seized and plundered by the insurgents. He led Charles I's forces against the rebels and in recognition of his loyal service, was elevated to the title Marquess of Ormond. Throughout the Irish Confederate Wars of the 1640s, he was the King's representative in Ireland. His castle, however, became the capital of the rebel Catholic Confederacy who had control of about two thirds of Ireland. In 1649 Charles I was executed, and the following year Oliver Cromwell invaded Ireland with his New Model Army. Cromwell besieged Kilkenny Castle in March 1650, and after five days of heavy fighting, the castle garrison surrendered.

The Marquess of Ormond left Ireland, joining Charles II in exile in France, where he became one of his most trusted advisers. When Charles II was restored as king, Ormond was elevated to Duke of Ormonde, made a privy counsellor and he returned to Ireland in 1662 as Lord Lieutenant.

At Kilkenny, Ormonde began rebuilding the castle, retaining the outline of the outer walls and towers, but giving it the appearance of a chateau he had admired in France. French artisans were used and stone was brought from Caen in Normandy where he had spent time in exile. In 1679, it was recorded that the courtyard was paved, the Duke's apartment nearly ready and that marble piers for the grotto, chimney pieces for the castle and 145 trees for the garden had arrived. Formal gardens were created with long avenues of oak and ash trees, terraces were made and statues ordered from the sculptor John Bonnier, which included life-size figures of Diana, the Sabine woman, the Roman hero Hercules, emperor Commodus and the Roman politician and general Antonius, as well as designs and emblems for the twelve signs of the zodiac and the four seasons. To the south-east of the castle a circular summer banqueting house was built that contained a large fountain. An inventory of the castle's contents taken at this time records over

(Clockwise from top): Library, original glazed bookcase at rear right, from which the others were reproduced; the Picture Gallery (*c.* 1900); the Picture Gallery today. The roof was elaborately decorated by J. H. Pollen, Professor of Fine Arts at Newman College, Dublin. *The Irish Builder* commented that 'the roof was probably intended to be Byzantine but is merely bizarre'.

100 rooms and gives an impression of taste and luxury. There were fine tapestries, lacquered and crystal sconces, chairs upholstered with silk brocade and figured velvet, japanned armchairs and cabinets, silk, velvet and damask hangings, looking glasses framed in silver and ebony or gilt, a cabinet inlaid with tortoiseshell, as well as many portraits, landscapes and paintings of biblical and classical subjects.

The first Duke of Ormonde died in 1688, and his grandson, also called James, became the second Duke and completed the castle, adding the magnificent entrance gateway on the south-west street front of the castle. The remodelling of the castle was, however, not favoured by all. Dr Molyneux, writing in 1709, said 'There is not one handsome or noble apartment. The Rooms are Darke, and the stairs mighty ugly.'

The second Duke was accused of supporting the Jacobite rising of 1715 and, like his grandfather, fled to France. The Parliament of Ireland passed an act declaring his estates and title forfeit and offered a reward of £10,000 for his capture. The same parliament, however, passed an act in 1721 allowing the Duke's brother, Charles Butler, first Earl of Arran, to purchase the Ormonde estate. His son, John, was recognised by parliament as the seventeenth Earl of Ormonde and lived in the castle until his death in 1795.

John's first son, Walter, the eighteenth Earl, gave up his hereditary right to the grant of the Prisage of Wine and received £216,000 from the government in compensation, about €20 million in today's money. In 1825, the second son, James, the nineteenth Earl, was made Marquess of Ormonde, the title being created for a second time. He was one of Ireland's richest landlords and, with no shortage of funds, he employed the architect William Robertson to remodel the castle.

In the 1670s, the Marquess of the first creation had tried to remove the castle's antique and fortified appearance and now the new Marquess tried to recreate it. The artist William Bartlett, who was in Kilkenny when work was in progress, wrote that the castle was being 'modernised within and unmodernised without'. The towers were built up and castellated, mock battlements and machicolations added, and the Picture Gallery built on the north side. Huge amounts were spent on the interiors and furnishing. Robertson's bill alone came to £30,815, about €3.5 million in today's money.

The Ormondes were not entirely pleased with Robertson's work and in the 1860s the Marchioness employed the architects Deane and Woodward to reroof the castle, remodel the Picture Gallery range with a new pitched roof and make alterations to the garden front of the castle.

In 1904, James Butler, the third Marquess of Ormonde, and his wife, Lady Elizabeth, entertained King Edward VII and Queen Alexandra at the castle. After a dinner party, there was a reception for 400 guests, held in the Picture Gallery.

The third Marquess was the last to live at Kilkenny Castle. Death duties and expenses following his death in 1919 amounted to £166,000. In 1935, the family gave up on the castle, and its contents were sold off in an auction that lasted ten days. Years of neglect followed and the castle fell increasingly into dereliction until 1967 when Arthur Butler, the sixth Marquess and twenty-fourth Earl of Ormonde, sold the castle to a restoration committee for £50. Shortly afterwards, it was handed over to the Irish state, and the OPW began a restoration programme that saw many areas of the castle interior totally rebuilt. Charles Butler, the seventh and last Marquess of Ormonde, died in 1997 aged ninety-eight, without a male heir. Today, Kilkenny Castle has been returned to its nineteenth-century splendour and is open to the public daily. (www.kilkennycastle.ie)

Kilwaughter Castle

County Antrim

(L–r): View of castle entrance; photograph of castle entrance (c. 1900). (*Courtesy F. Rawlin*)

THE AGNEW FAMILY first arrived on the Kilwaughter estate, near Larne in County Antrim, in the late twelfth century. In 1177, Philip d'Agneaux was one of the twenty-two Norman knights who came north into Ulster with John de Courcy, where d'Agneaux was awarded the lordship of Larne. A little to the north of the present ruined castle stands a motte, probably once crowned by Philip's wooden keep, forming a typical Norman motte-and-bailey castle.

Lord Agnew supported the 1315 invasion into Ireland of Edward Bruce, and after Edward's 1318 defeat and death at the Battle of Faughart, was rewarded for his loyalty by being created Constable of Lochnaw, the impregnable fortress of Edward's brother, King Robert Bruce of Scotland. Lord Agnew relocated to Scotland, where the family flourished. He was created Sheriff of Wigtown, a lucrative hereditary post that was held for twelve generations. Back in Ireland, the Kilwaughter estate was left in the hands of various family members and tenants until 1576, when Sorley Boy MacDonnell seized most of the Antrim's coastal lands, including the Agnew estate. Sorley Boy's son, Randal (see Dunluce Castle, p. 96) was created Earl of Antrim in 1620, and in 1634 he signed a lease of the Kilwaughter estate back to Sir Patrick Agnew, for the annual sum of £20. Sir Patrick remained in Scotland, whilst another family member, Captain Patrick Agnew, resided at Kilwaughter where he built a modest four-storey T-plan castle in the Scottish style. A restored similar castle can be seen nearby at Ballygally, which forms part of the Ballygally Castle Hotel.

These were troubled times and the primary purpose of Captain Agnew's castle was defence. It was surrounded by a stout bawn wall and the castle's windows were narrow slits, designed for firing out arrows or muskets rather than allowing in much light. The Irish Rebellion of 1641 caused a major shake-up of the district and rather than test the castle's strength, the Scottish and English settlers of the Kilwaughter estate fled to Larne for refuge. Larne was hurriedly fortified, with Captain Agnew placed in charge of its defence. It was more than ten years later, after Cromwell's bloody campaign, that the Agnews could return to Kilwaughter and begin restoring the estate to prosperity.

Most of the Agnews' firstborn sons were named Patrick, creating something of a genealogical headache. In 1708, Patrick Agnew, great-grandson of Patrick, the builder of the castle, bought out the interests of the Scottish Agnews, converting Kilwaughter into a freehold property. During the eighteenth century, the estate saw various improvements. As the castle's defensive purpose became less important, its windows were enlarged. Patrick and his wife, Jenny, began laying out a deer park, as recorded in a tablet embedded into the estate's boundary wall: 'This work was begun by Patrick Agnew and Jenny Shaw in Seventeen Hundred and Twenty Two.' Patrick was followed by his son, another Patrick, and then his son, William, who inherited the Kilwaughter estate in the middle of the eighteenth century.

William married Margaret Steward of Killymoon Castle, which would later influence the redesign of Kilwaughter Castle. William became High Sheriff of County Antrim in 1774.

William and Margaret had two sons, James and William, who both died young, and two daughters, Maria and Jane. Maria, the eldest daughter, first married James Ross, a successful banker and merchant involved in trade with the West Indies. After the death of her first husband, Maria married his business partner, Valentine Jones, one of the early builders of Belfast and an extremely successful banker and wine merchant trading with the West Indies. Through the marriage Valentine also acquired a large portion of his former business partner's wealth. Their son, Edward, eventually inherited Kilwaughter, from his grandfather, William, and as a condition, took the additional surname of Agnew, becoming Edward Jones Agnew.

Edward, like his father, became a very successful merchant. He was also MP for County Antrim in the Irish Parliament from 1792 to 1797 and High Sheriff of County Antrim in 1803. In 1802, Edward's cousin, William Stewart, employed John Nash, one of London's leading architects, to design and rebuild Killymoon Castle after the original castle was destroyed in a fire. In 1806, Edward's father died, leaving him a considerable inheritance. This, combined with Nash's success at Killymoon, seems to have prompted Edward to also employ Nash to redesign and extend Kilwaughter Castle.

Nash was a master of picturesque neo-Gothic castles, the first of which was probably his own residence, East Cowes Castle on the Isle of Wight. He received many Irish commissions such as the similar Lough Cutra Castle (see p. 158) in County Galway and Shanbally Castle in County Tipperary (totally demolished in 1960). Nash later became the personal architect of George IV, designing much of London's finest architecture, including Buckingham Palace and Regent's Park.

At Kilwaughter, Nash's design was reasonably modest, comprising a total of thirty-four rooms. Typical of his castles, Kilwaughter comprises an asymmetrical combination of conjoined crenulated blocks of various storey heights, including square, circular and octagonal towers. The earlier T-plan castle was incorporated and its Scottish influence

Entrance hall, doorway to circular tower at centre.

(Clockwise from top left): Drawing room in circular tower 2016; view from basement looking up into castle interior; drawing room in circular tower (c. 1900). (*Courtesy F. Rawlin*)

retained by Nash who extended its corbelled corner bartizan turrets. Nash has often been accused of poor workmanship and inattention to detail, and some elements of his work at Kilwaughter have been accused of being shoddy, such as the rectangular sash windows that were masked externally with timber Gothic tracery, and some of the roofs, which were finished with only sand and tar. Other elements of Kilwaughter, however, show a high degree of craftsmanship, such as the elaborately carved sandstone windowsills.

The process of remodelling begun by Nash continued until at least 1830, when an oriel window was added to the east side of the castle. Millar and Nelson, architects of Belfast, were employed to carry out other additions, including a single-storey library block to the west, and a gatehouse that was built alongside Nash's original entrance gate.

Edward Jones Agnew died in 1834, leaving Kilwaughter to his ten-year-old son, William. The estate was managed by Edward's unmarried sister, Margaret, until her death in 1848, and then by the young William. The census of 1851 records Kilwaughter occupied by William, aged twenty-six, his land agent, John Lambert, and the house staff of a butler, housekeeper, cook, footman, three housemaids and a kitchen maid. Other staff on the estate included a ploughman, farm labourers, a gardener and a gamekeeper. A few years later the estate is recorded as amounting to 9,770 acres.

Circular tower with elaborate carved windowsill at bottom.

William never married and in his later years spent most of his time in Paris. When he died in 1891, Kilwaughter was inherited by his niece, Countess Maria Balzani, the daughter of William's sister, who had married Count Ugo Balzani, a distinguished Italian historian. The Balzanis had little use for an Irish castle and Kilwaughter was let to a relative and business acquaintance of the Agnews, John Galt Smith, a successful Belfast linen merchant, who traded with America and spent most of his time in New York.

Smith's first wife, Cornelia Knapp, died in 1883, leaving him with two daughters. He married again, in 1886, this time to Elizabeth 'Bessie' Shipley Bringhurst, who was twenty years his junior. Elizabeth's father was the successful millionaire businessman Edward Bringhurst Jr, who lived in Rockwood, an English-style country estate in Wilmington, Delaware, USA. The couple divided their time between New York City and Ireland, where they first lived in Meadowbank, a house in north Belfast, before signing a thirty-year lease on Kilwaughter.

John Galt Smith died in 1899. Bessie continued to live at Kilwaughter during the summer months and in 1903 she was presented to the Royal Court of King Edward VII at Dublin Castle. She travelled to Ireland in June 1914, and became stranded owing to the onset of hostilities leading to the First World War. Being unable to book safe passage back to America until 1919, she made best use of the war years by offering the castle to be used as a hospital for wounded officers. At the end of the First World War the escalating Irish Civil War prompted Bessie to vacate Kilwaughter. She brought many possessions back to America, and much of the castle's remaining furniture and contents were sold at auction. She moved back to Delaware in 1922, and lived at Rockwood for the remainder of her life, where she and her sister, Mary, entertained many guests with frequent dinner parties.

In the preceding years most of the Kilwaughter estate lands had been sold off under the 1903 Land Act. The castle was inherited by Count Ugo and Countess Maria Balzani's two daughters, Gwendoline and Nora, who both lived in Italy. Because of this Italian connection, on the outbreak of the Second World War the castle was declared Enemy Property. The Custodian of Enemy Property for Northern Ireland ordered a sale of the castle's furnishings, and it was then requisitioned for use by the military, and used to billet members of the American 644th Tank Destroyer Battalion preparing for D-Day.

After the war, Kilwaughter was left unoccupied and in poor condition. Following several more years of deterioration, in 1951 it was purchased by E. H. McConnell (Metals) Ltd of Belfast who proceeded to strip the castle of its lead roofs, woodwork, slates and anything else of value. Thereafter the castle was abandoned. In 1982, the remaining property was sold by Bianca Balzani, the next of kin of Gwendoline and Nora Balzani.

The present owners have formed the Kilwaughter Castle Restoration Group, which is working with heritage bodies to try to stabilise or restore the building from its present perilous condition.

Kilwaughter Castle is located on private property and is not open to the public.

King John's Castle

County Limerick

THIS IMPOSING CASTLE, known as King John's, lies on the eastern bank of the River Shannon in the north-west part of Limerick city. It was built in the early thirteenth century by the Anglo-Normans to protect the crossing point to Thomond. Partly constructed on an earlier twelfth-century ring work, the castle lay to the north of the original Viking settlement, Ostman, and was incorporated into the growing town walls. The annals mention a bawn here in 1200 and a castle two years later. There is no evidence that King John had a direct hand in the castle's building, but it became a royal castle after 1211, when he ordered it put into the hands of the Lord Justice.

The castle has no keep, and its strength is derived from a huge curtain wall enclosing a courtyard with large circular towers at each angle. A large gate building with two D-shaped towers was built on the northern side, where the entrance was protected by a drawbridge and portcullis.

The King appointed the castle's constables and there is an uninterrupted line of people holding this office from the appointment of Godfrey de Roche in 1216 until the death of Viscount Gort in 1842, when an Act of Parliament abolished the position. Sir John Wogan, the Justiciar of Ireland, visited Limerick in 1312 and was horrified at the state in which he found the castle, recording it in a letter to be 'threatened with ruin and so broken down on all sides and fallen down that peril may arise if it is not soon repaired and unless turrets and crennels be constructed'. Work on the castle was completed the following year but it was not enough to prevent a mass escape from the castle gaol in 1318. Another jailbreak occurred in 1332, when the Earl of Desmond's men were imprisoned in the castle. They managed to escape their cell, murder the constable and then take control of the castle. The mayor and his citizens, however, soon regained the castle and the Desmond men were put to death.

From 1450, Limerick rarely features in official records and as time went on its connection with the English government became purely nominal. By the early years of the sixteenth century the citizens had begun to look after their own defences and a description of the city from the historian Richard Stanihurst in 1577 records it as 'having sumptuous and substantial buildings and a quay where ships of 200 tons may berth'.

Aerial view from south-west.

(L–r): Interior view of castle entrance; view along curtain walls to entrance tower.

In 1600, repairs to the castle were ordered by the Lord President of Munster, Sir George Carew. The English military engineer Sir Josias Bodley completed the work in 1611. He replaced the south-east corner tower with a bastion capable of carrying five or six guns as well as strengthening the other towers which had been undermined by water.

In 1642, the castle's constable, Captain George Courtenay, with a garrison of sixty of his own men, twenty-eight warders and about a hundred others, defended the castle against an attack by Irish Catholic Confederate troops. About 600 English Protestant settlers had taken refuge in the castle to escape the Irish Rebellion that had begun in the previous year. Most of the city's population was Catholic and welcomed the Catholic Confederate troops who were under the command of Garrett Barry. Without sufficient troops or expertise to take the castle by assault, Barry fell back on an old siege tactic: using men from his army and miners from Tipperary, as well as the city's citizens, he set to work digging tunnels under the castle in an effort to undermine its walls. A day-by-day account of the following weeks was recorded by a cleric, Ambrose Jones. On 17 June he wrote: 'This morning was perceived a great cracke in the bulwarke of our castle from the top to ye bottome which before we doubted to be undermined.' A few days later a tunnel under the northern wall of the castle was collapsed, bringing down one corner of the castle walls. Caught between a choice of a fight to the death or surrender, the castle's defenders laid down their arms and marched out.

In 1651, the castle was surrendered to the Parliamentary General Ireton who had bombarded it from the foot of the nearby Thomond Bridge. In 1691, the castle was again the scene of dramatic events when it was surrendered by Jacobite hero Patrick Sarsfield to the Williamites. Under the subsequent signing of the Treaty of Limerick (reputedly carried out on the Treaty Stone, a limestone block which is today mounted on a pedestal opposite the castle), the English promised to respect the civilian population of Limerick, to tolerate the Catholic religion in Ireland and to allow Sarsfield and the Jacobite army to withdraw to France. Later, it was said that the ink was not dry on the treaty when the English broke it.

In 1787, a barracks was built inside the castle, so continuing its military function until 1935, when Limerick Corporation took down part of the castle wall and erected twenty-two houses in the courtyard. These houses were demolished in 1989 when the castle was restored as a tourist attraction. The latest addition to the structure is the interpretative centre, which allows visitors to view an underground area excavated in the 1990s, revealing the tunnels dug under the castle walls in the 1642 siege. The tunnels were found well preserved with wooden props and side-wall lining planks still in place. King John's Castle is open to the public daily from April to December.

Kylemore Abbey

County Galway

(Above): Kylemore Abbey entrance front; (right): an angel holding a shield bearing the Henry coat of arms, positioned over the entrance doorway.

KYLEMORE CASTLE was built by Mitchell Henry in 1867. It was bought by Benedictine nuns in 1920, and thereafter known as Kylemore Abbey. Mitchell Henry was a medical surgeon of Irish parentage and living in London, with a practice on the prestigious Harley Street. His father, Alexander Henry, was an extremely successful merchant whose company, A. & S. Henry, was the main exporter trading between England and America, Brazil, Australia and the South Seas Islands. When Alexander died in 1862, he left almost £700,000 in assets, more than €100 million in today's money. Mitchell soon gave up his medical career and became chairman of A. & S. Henry. He did not engage directly with the day-to-day running of the company, but oversaw and directed its operations. Mitchell became one of the wealthiest men in the country. As well as a vast inheritance, through his father's company and various investments he received an annual income of over £60,000, in those days a very significant sum.

Mitchell married an Irishwoman, Margaret Vaughan, and they honeymooned in Connemara. He was a keen sportsman and in the following years he often returned to take advantage of the region's renowned fishing. Soon after taking over his father's company, Mitchell began remodelling two properties, Stratheden House in London, which would become the family's London residence, and Kylemore Lodge in Galway, which he had purchased after leasing it during his previous Connemara fishing holidays.

From 1863, Mitchell began acquiring various parcels of land around Kylemore and within a few years he had amassed a large fishing and shooting estate amounting to 15,615 acres at a total cost of a little over £18,000. Much of the land was very poor quality and uneconomical to farm; however, Mitchell spared no expense as he began a vast campaign of land reclamation and improvement. His work transformed the productivity of the land, the lives of his tenants and the beauty of the region, but it would ultimately end in his own financial ruin forty years later.

On 4 September 1867, the first stone of Kylemore Castle was laid. The castle was designed by Samuel Ussher Roberts, who had recently completed Gurteen Castle in County Waterford. Many features used at Gurteen were also used at Kylemore, and the same builder, Thomas Carroll, worked on both castles. The plasterwork was carried out by the well-respected James Hogan & Sons of Dublin, and the stonecutter was M. O'Brien of Ballinasloe.

The new castle was built as a colossal extension to the existing lodge house and was designed so that Mitchell's staff could remain living in the lodge during its construction. The work provided vast employment in the area with more than 100 men well paid for their labour. Construction of the walled garden, by far the largest in Ireland, as well as the laying-out of pleasure grounds and two miles of walks, also went on simultaneously. The work took four years to complete. The construction costs of the castle amounted to a little over £29,000, but in total Mitchell is thought to have spent more than half a million pounds on the entire estate, about €60 million in today's money.

Comprising seventy rooms spread out over 40,000 square feet (over 3,700 square metres), Kylemore Castle dwarfed all other residences in Connemara. Nothing came anywhere near to it in terms of size or grandeur. The interior of the building was completely changed in subsequent years, but descriptions and family photographs record its initial opulence. Inside the Gothic entrance, crowned by an angel holding a shield bearing the Henry coat of arms, were four spacious halls, all leading one into another through Gothic arches supported by pillars of Connemara marble. The floors were of polished oak and the walls and ceiling panelled with deep mouldings. The staircase was of oak, with a mahogany handrail, and was lit by a richly decorated stained-glass window. On the north side of the staircase hall was the gallery

Drawing room.

Dining room.

hall, often used for dancing and games. Leading off the halls was a suite of magnificent reception rooms, including the drawing room, morning room, breakfast room, dining room, library, study and saloon, all designed for entertaining on a lavish and extensive scale. Stairs to the rear of the saloon led to the billiard room, ballroom and access to the domestic quarters. There were thirty-three bedrooms distributed across the eastern wing, western wing and the Venetian wing, which contained the 'bachelor's quarters', eight bedrooms to the rear of the castle apparently designed to offer privacy.

The servants' wing contained a further four shared bedrooms, while the butler, cook and housekeeper all had their own bedrooms. Other rooms included a schoolroom, smoking room, gunroom, workrooms, a linen room, storerooms, kitchen, scullery, and still room, a meat larder, fish larder and vegetable larder, plate room, brushing room, china room, beer cellar, Turkish bathhouse, coal room and lamp room.

Nothing was spared in the cost of the castle's interior, which included all modern conveniences and the latest technologies of the time, such as indoor plumbing, gas lighting, electricity supplied by a water turbine, service lifts to the upper floors and fire hydrants. Kylemore had its own fire brigade staffed by volunteers who were very proud of their response times. The only fire they ever had to deal with, however, was in their station house, which was destroyed because they were unable to get to their hoses and pump to fight the blaze.

Mitchell and his wife, Margaret, had five daughters and four sons. They lived like royalty, dividing their time between London and Kylemore. In 1874, whilst holidaying in Egypt, Margaret contracted a fever and died a few days later. She was just forty-five years old, and left young children: Violet (two years old) and Florence (four years old). Mitchell retreated to Ireland where he employed the architect James Franklin Fuller to build a memorial chapel about a mile from the castle on the shore of the lake. Here Margaret was finally laid to rest and in due course Mitchell would join her. Their eldest daughter took over the running of the family, assisted by various tutors and nannies.

Margaret Mitchell (1829–1874). Originally a full length portrait, it was cut down to fit the home of her second-youngest daughter, Florence, in Bunaboghee House near Letterfrack. The portrait was later returned to Kylemore after Florence's death in 1959.

In 1892, an incident occurred which would have another dramatic effect on Mitchell. During a family excursion from the castle, his 32-year-old daughter Geraldine was driving an open carriage with her baby daughter and nursemaid, whilst others were in another carriage ahead of them. As they approached the Derryinver Bridge, a few miles from the castle, the horse began to bolt and then shied, throwing the carriage's occupants out onto the road. The baby and nursemaid were not hurt but initially Geraldine could not be found. Her lifeless body was eventually recovered from the nearby river several hours later. Within a year, Mitchell had left A. & S. Henry and put Kylemore up for sale.

No buyer was forthcoming and it soon became evident that the family money was beginning to run out. In 1901 there were outstanding mortgages of £93,000 on Stratheden House and £57,000 on Kylemore. Stratheden House in London was sold and its contents auctioned off. Kylemore was left in the hands of Mitchell's youngest son, Lorenzo, who lived in the seventy-room castle pretty much by himself. Mitchell retired to the Regent Hotel in Leamington Spa, England, where he died on 22 November 1910, leaving just £425. His body was cremated and his ashes brought back to Kylemore to lie beside his wife.

In 1903, Kylemore was purchased by the Duke and Duchess of Manchester for the bargain price of £63,000. The Duke had inherited a heavily indebted estate from his father who had died when he was still a minor. He had a reputation of being a rakish playboy and gambler, and maintained an extremely lavish lifestyle, as a result of which he was bankrupt by the age of twenty-three. The purchase of Kylemore was funded by his wife's wealthy father, the American businessman Eugene Zimmerman. The couple soon made many changes at Kylemore, removing much of the Connemara marble, remodelling the interiors and changing the layout of many bedrooms. They entertained extravagantly and within a few years were also having financial difficulties. They left Kylemore in 1914, after the death of the Duchess's father.

In 1920, Kylemore was purchased by a community of Benedictine nuns whose abbey in Ypres, Belgium, had been destroyed in the early days of the First World War. The nuns ran a farm at Kylemore, opened a guesthouse, established an international boarding school and later a day school. In the day school, local girls were offered an education free of charge. The principal reception rooms were converted into classrooms and other rooms converted into dormitories. The guesthouse was closed following a devastating fire in 1959. Dwindling numbers of nuns and increased running costs eventually led to the closure of the school, with the last students sitting their exams in June 2010.

Today, Kylemore is a centre for retreat activities as well as being used by Notre Dame University of Indiana, USA. There is also a heavy focus on tourism. Much of the castle's interior has been returned to its former grandeur and is open to the public. Kylemore Abbey, its grounds, walks and gardens now form a highlight of a trip to Connemara. Kylemore Abbey is open to the public daily throughout the year. (www.kylemoreabbey.com)

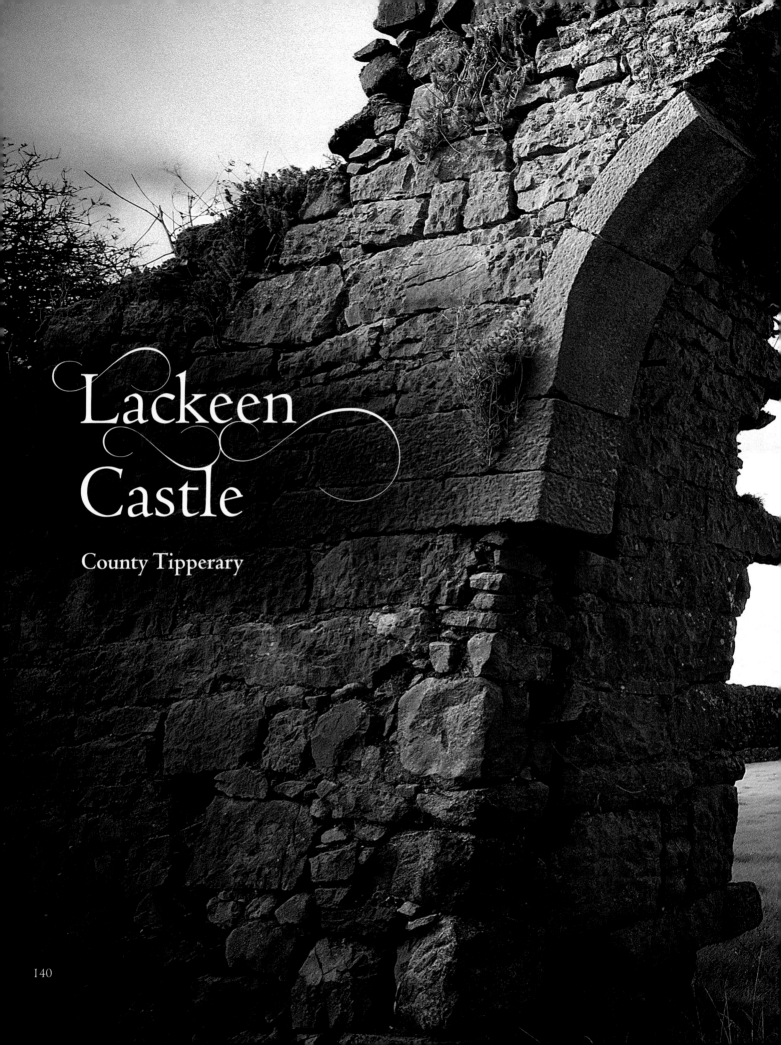

Lackeen
Castle

County Tipperary

Mural stairs leading to first floor.

View from first floor looking down.

LACKEEN WAS HOME of the Ua Cinnéide chieftains, described in the Annals of the Four Masters as being 'the undisputed Lords of Ormond' by the end of the twelfth century. The name Ua Cinnéide can be translated as 'of the Helmeted Head', a name given to the clan as they were the first to wear helmets in battle against the Vikings. The Cinnéides split into three branches, the chiefs of which were referred to by their hair colour: *Donn* (brown), *Fionn* (blond), and *Rua* (red). Lackeen Castle was built by Brian Ua Cinnéide Fionn in the sixteenth century.

Lackeen Castle is a four-storey tower surrounded by a large bawn. The bawn is entered through a round-arched gateway, where there was probably once a gatehouse. The tower doorway, in its southern wall, was protected by a machicolation at roof level, from where rocks and other missiles could be thrown down on unwelcome visitors. There is also a horizontal slit overhanging the external face of the door, from where boiling oil could be poured down directly over the enemy's heads. If attackers managed to get through the tower door, they could also be attacked with arrows or other missiles from a murder hole in the ceiling of the entrance lobby. A straight mural staircase leads up to the first-floor level, where the floor was made of timber and does not survive. From the first floor, spiral stairs, also protected by a murder hole, then lead up to the main hall, located on the second floor, a third floor, and up to the battlemented wall-walk.

After the death of Brian in 1588, the castle passed to his son, Donnchadh, who further fortified it against the Cromwellian forces, but ended up surrendering to Cromwell in 1653. The Cinnéides later regained their lands, and in time their name became anglicised to O'Kennedy and Kennedy.

Second-floor side chamber.

Entrance to spiral staircase.

Third-floor main chamber.

John O'Kennedy rebuilt and restored the castle in 1735 and, in the process, discovered a magnificent illuminated manuscript hidden in its walls. It was written mostly in Latin but also with some Gaelic, in about AD 750, making it one of the oldest books of its kind in Europe. It was acquired by the Duke of Buckingham for the Stowe manuscript collection, and became known as the Stowe Missal. The manuscript is now in the Royal Irish Academy in Dublin.

By 1800, members of the Kennedy family had dispersed across Ireland and had also emigrated to America where the most famous member of the family in modern times was the 35th President of the United States, John F. Kennedy.

Legend states that Lackeen Castle is haunted by Kennedy's Phooka, a fairy shape-shifter capable of assuming a variety of terrifying forms, usually a horse or goat. The story goes that O'Kennedy managed to catch the Phooka, shortly after completing the castle. Bound up in ropes, with a sword at its throat, the Phooka was made to swear an oath never to harm or hinder any member of the Kennedy family. The Phooka can apparently still be seen wandering the castle grounds on dark nights. Its favourite trick is to sneak up slowly, then throw his head between a man's legs, whisking him off his feet and up on to his back. He then flies up to the moon, or down to the bottom of a lake, or over an ocean, all the time with the rider hanging on for dear life.

Today, Lackeen Castle is a National Monument in the ownership of the Irish state, and is freely open to the public.

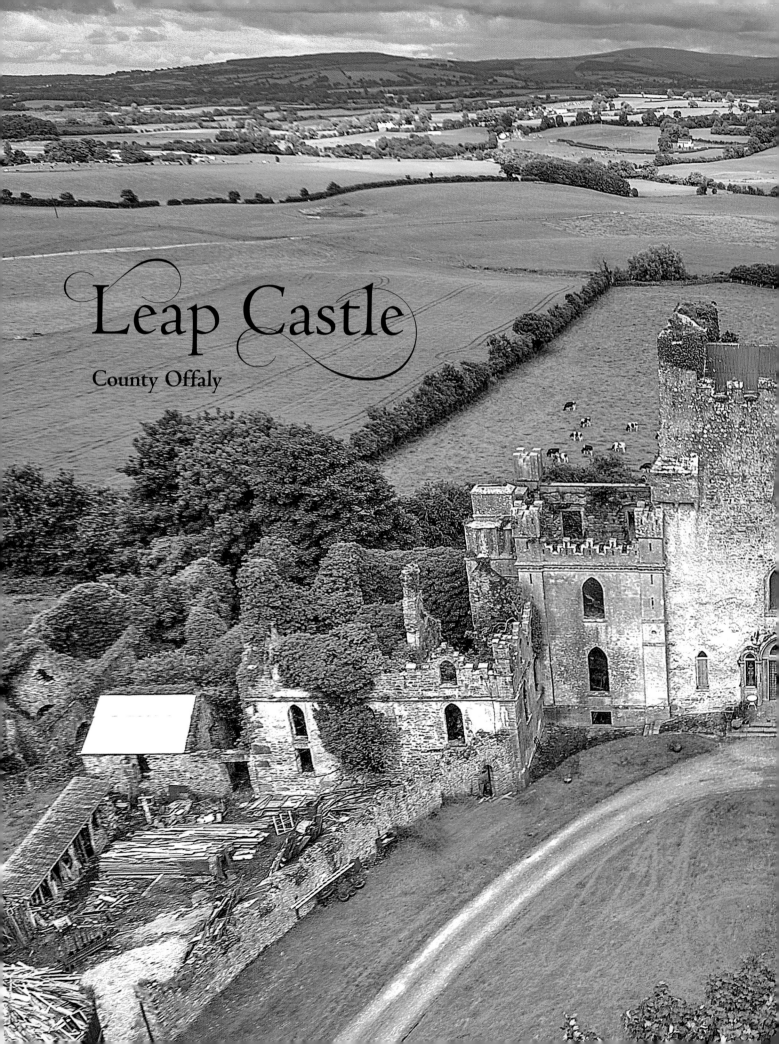

Leap Castle

County Offaly

(Clockwise from top left): Lithograph of castle (*c.* 1800); Sean Ryan at the castle entrance; first-floor hall.

L EAP CASTLE STANDS on a vast rock guarding a strategic pass through the Slieve Bloom Mountains. In the sixteenth century, the castle was the main stronghold of the O'Carrolls, fierce and powerful Irish chieftains who ruled over the surrounding territory of Ely, and termed themselves 'Princes of Ely'.

John O'Carroll began building the castle around the middle of the fifteenth century, and when he died of the plague in 1489, his son, Mulroney O'Carroll, became head of the O'Carroll clan and continued with its construction. Mulroney was described in the Annals of the Four Masters as 'the most distinguished man of his time for renown,

Painting on interior wall (not original).

valour, prosperity and excellence, to whom poets, travellers, ecclesiastics and literary men were most thankful'. When he died in 1532 a bitter and bloody fight for Leap Castle and the leadership of the O'Carroll clan erupted between cousins, illegitimate sons and namesakes, which lasted nearly 100 years. Mulroney's illegitimate son, Fearganainm (which translates from Irish as 'man without name') first seized control and became involved in a vicious dispute with another local clan, the O'Mulloys. During a feast held at Leap an entire party of the O'Mulloys was murdered at the castle dinner table. In revenge the O'Mulloys slaughtered Fearganainm at Clonlisk Castle a few weeks later. Fearganainm's son, Thady, 'the One-Eyed', and his cousin Charles then took control of Leap. Thady was awarded the title Lord Baron of Ely, but his now-jealous cousin assassinated him a few months later. Charles, in turn, was murdered by his brother, William 'The Pale', who ruled over Ely from 1554. William had a relatively long reign of twenty-seven years before being slain by the O'Connors. William's son, John, then assumed control but was quickly murdered by his cousin Mulroney, son of One-Eyed Thady. John's murder was then revenged by his illegitimate brother, Charles, who did away with Mulroney.

Charles was accepted as chief by the English, knighted in 1586, but murdered in another feud in 1600. Four O'Carrolls now competed for leadership and the clan was split into quarters. Eventually the Commission for the Plantation of Ely O'Carroll declared the territory Crown property and introduced English settlers in an effort to promote stability.

Following the Cromwellian land confiscations, Leap Castle was awarded to Jonathan Darby, one of Cromwell's soldiers of fortune. The castle then remained in the hands of the Darby family for about 350 years, throughout which nearly all of the Darby firstborn sons were named Jonathan. In about 1750, the fifth Jonathan Darby remodelled the castle as his mansion house, adding Gothic wings to the north and south sides of the earlier castle. A few years later Leap was described as 'a most beautiful seat, and fine castle, with noble and extensive demesnes, plantations and walks'.

Construction works were continued by many of the successive Darbys until the early 1900s when workmen found an oubliette, a trapdoor through which prisoners were pushed to their deaths. In the underground dungeon below, the grim discovery was made of approximately 150 human skeletons, evidence of the brutal, murderous activities carried out in the castle during the O'Carrolls' tenure several centuries earlier. Three full cartloads of bones and skulls were removed from the dungeon. The Lord of Leap at that time, Jonathan Charles Darby, also made the gruesome discovery of three upright skeletons sealed into one of the internal castle walls. He immediately ordered them bricked up, believing his ancestors must have had good reason to put them there in the first place.

It was about this time that Leap's reputation for being by far the most haunted castle in Western Europe began to take root. Darby's wife, Mildred (or, as she preferred to be called, Milly), began dabbling in the occult and held a number of séances at the castle. This seemed to initiate numerous bizarre happenings that were recorded by Milly in the December 1908 edition of the magazine *Occult Review*.

Milly wrote about a creature that appeared to many of the castle's visitors called 'the Thing', 'the Elemental' or

First-floor side chamber.

(L–r): The second-floor 'bloody chapel'; the oubliette, from where three full cartloads of bones and skulls were removed; derelict north wing.

just 'IT'. She described her own encounter with the creature thus: 'Suddenly, two hands were laid on my shoulders. I turned around sharply and saw … a grey 'Thing' standing a couple of feet from me, with its bent arms raised, as if it were cursing me … so sinister, repulsive and devilish. My friends who are clever about occult things say it is what they call an 'Elemental'.

Other ghostly spectres included the apparition of a tall lady dressed entirely in red, with her hand holding a knife or dagger, raised menacingly in the air, and a dark monk-like figure wearing a black habit.

Milly and her husband's time at Leap was cut short during the Troubles of 1922. On the night of 30 July, when the couple were away, IRA irregulars broke into the castle, bringing with them thirty bombs and twenty cases of petrol. They first got into the wine cellar, where they became so inebriated that they were unable to discharge the bombs and only managed to burn down a small part of the castle. They returned the following evening to complete their task. Anything that survived the inferno was then looted by locals.

Leap Castle remained a gaunt burnt-out ruin for over fifty years. In the mid-1930s, following an argument over several unexplained happenings witnessed in the castle before the fire, Jonathan Charles Darby challenged a man to spend just one night in the ruin, for which he would pay him £1,000. The man bedded down for the night with blankets, candles and a bottle of wine for company, but stayed less than an hour before he was seen running away, screaming for his life. He later refused to divulge any details of what had so struck him with terror.

In 1974, the ruin was brought by Peter Bartlett, an Australian with family connections to its early inhabitants. He had it exorcised and then began to restore the castle. Following his death in 1989, Leap was brought by the Ryans who continued with its restoration, transforming it into their fine family home.

Sean Ryan opens the castle to visitors and provides guided tours. He describes frequent interactions with Leap's otherworldly inhabitants, such as receiving numerous prods and pokes from invisible hands and hearing sounds of merriment, shrieks and shouts from empty rooms.

Lismore Castle

County Waterford

(Above): View inside courtyard facing north; (right): the Boyle arms and motto 'God's providence is our inheritance', over courtyard entrance.

LISMORE DERIVES ITS NAME from the Irish '*lios mór*', meaning 'great fort', originating from a Bronze Age fort located on a hill about a kilometre east of the present town. A settlement at Lismore was founded by St Carthage in the seventh century, which flourished to become one of the great Irish centres of religious learning. In 1171, Henry II landed at Waterford and travelled to Lismore, where he met a council of bishops. After the meeting he ordered the building of a castle, before going on to Cashel. Henry's castle was destroyed when the town was ransacked by the Anglo-Normans two years later, but was rebuilt by his son, Prince John, in 1185. The castle was again destroyed, this time by the native Irish, but was rebuilt and remained in use by bishops as an episcopal palace throughout the Middle Ages.

The origins of the present Lismore estate lie in the Munster Plantation of the late sixteenth century. Following the unsuccessful rebellion of Gerald FitzGerald, fifteenth Earl of Desmond in 1579, sections of his estate were granted to British settlers. In 1586, the largest portion, comprising over 42,000 acres concentrated around the fertile lower reaches of the River Blackwater, was granted to Sir Walter Raleigh, who had participated in the suppression of the rebellion. At this time, the castle at Lismore was in ruins and Raleigh based himself at Youghal. Raleigh had limited success with his Irish estates and in 1602 he sold the estate to Richard Boyle, later Earl of Cork, for £1,500.

(Clockwise from top left): Entrance hall; first drawing room; second drawing room.

Boyle had arrived in Ireland in 1588 aged twenty-two, with little more than the clothes he stood in and £27 in his pocket. The purchase of Raleigh's estate was funded in part by his marriage to Catherine, daughter of Sir Geoffrey Fenton, who brought a dowry of £1,000. Boyle, like Raleigh, first lived at Youghal, but soon began rebuilding, enlarging and embellishing Lismore Castle and after 1610 it became his principal residence. The castle courtyard was surrounded by three-storey gabled ranges, which joined the medieval corner towers. The principal rooms ran along the side above the Blackwater River, with the parlour and dining room in a wing that projected out over the edge of the precipice. Here an oriel window opened to a sheer drop down to the river below. On the far side from the river, Boyle built a gatehouse that incorporated a Romanesque arch dating from the earlier bishop's residence. Boyle's account books and diaries record numerous works at the castle such as the engagement of a stonecutter to 'make and

Nineteenth-century 'Medieval banqueting-hall' by Crace and Pugin.

carve four arms and crests with the corners in freestone' and 'two glasurs' who were paid for putting the staircase and schoolhouse 'into colours', and a plasterer who was engaged 'to ceil with fretwork my study, my bed chamber, and the nursery and to wash them with Spanish white'. Inventories of the castle interior record the walls being hung with tapestries, and embroidered silk and velvet. The castle gardens were also landscaped, with stout walls being added for defence as well as ornament.

Boyle's career was spectacular. He not only acquired one of the largest and richest estates in Ireland, but also attained high office, rising through the positions of clerk to the Presidential Council of Munster in 1600, Irish Privy Counsellor in 1613, Member of Parliament for Lismore in 1614, Lord Justice of Ireland in 1629, and Lord High Treasurer of Ireland in 1631. He was knighted in 1603, created Baron of Youghal in 1616, and advanced to the earldom of Cork in 1620. He continued to buy and receive grants of numerous landholdings, and by 1640 the annual rental income of all his estates amounted to more than £18,000, well over €3 million in today's money.

In 1626, Robert Boyle, the founder of modern chemistry, was born in Lismore Castle. He is well known for his experimental gas law, Boyle's Law, which states that for a fixed mass of gas at constant temperature, the volume is inversely proportional to the pressure. In 1642, another son, Roger Boyle, Baron Broghill, later first Earl of Orrery, defended the castle against a force of 5,000 rebels. He wrote to his father, who had removed to Youghal for safety: 'My Lord, fear nothing for Lismore; for if it be lost, it shall be with the life of him, that begs your Lordship's blessing, and stiles himself your Lordship's most humble, most obliged, and most dutiful son and servant.'

The first Earl died in 1643, leaving behind a small empire and a dynasty that would dominate the economy, society, and politics of Munster for the next century. His estate was split between his sons, with Richard, the eldest, becoming the second Earl of Cork and inheriting most of the Cork and Waterford estates, which amounted to over 90,000 acres.

The castle was attacked again in 1645 – this time it was badly damaged – and then taken by the Confederate Catholics under Lord Castlehaven. The second Earl had the castle patched up and the story goes that James II stayed a night here in 1689 and almost fainted when he looked out of the dining-room window and saw the great drop to the river below. The second Earl lived principally in England, whilst still making regular visits to his Irish estates. In 1664, he was created Earl of Burlington, and built Burlington House in Piccadilly, London. In 1682, he purchased an estate at Chiswick in Middlesex, which then became his permanent residence. The Irish estates, however, remained the principal source of the families' wealth, bringing in an annual income of £30,000 (about €5 million today) by the 1670s.

Subsequently, the Burlington estates in England became of more interest to the second Earl's heirs. Their Irish lands remained a lucrative source of income, but their management was lax and corruption was rife. On the death of Richard, fourth Earl of Cork, in 1753, the Cork title devolved on a kinsman, and Lismore Castle and about 40,000 acres went to his only surviving daughter, Charlotte. She was married to William Cavendish, the fourth Duke of Devonshire, who owned a vast landed estate in Derbyshire and Yorkshire, including Chatsworth House, Hardwick Hall and Bolton Abbey. The fifth Duke of Devonshire took more interest in his Irish inheritance and built a new bridge across the Blackwater at Lismore in 1775. Little, however, was done to the castle and in 1787 it was described as a 'venerable ruin'. A painting by Thomas Sautelle Roberts at the end of the eighteenth century also shows the castle in ruins.

In 1811, William Spencer Cavendish succeeded as sixth Duke of Devonshire. Often referred to as the Bachelor Duke, he set about transforming the castle into a fashionable fortress and it soon became his favourite residence. From 1812 to 1822, the architect William Atkinson was employed to rebuild the castle at a cost of £43,000, in those days a very considerable sum of money. The castle's two main drawing rooms are essentially as Atkinson left them; however, much of the castle's present appearance is the result of a second phase of rebuilding.

In 1850, in the Duke's latter years, he employed the architect Sir Joseph Paxton, designer of the Crystal Palace in Hyde Park, London, to carry out extensive improvements and additions. Paxton used ready-cut stone, shipped over from Derbyshire in England. The leading maker of Gothic Revival furniture, John Gregory Crace of London, and his partner, the leading architect Pugin, were commissioned to transform the ruined chapel of the old bishop's palace into a medieval banqueting hall and it was given the full-blown ecclesiastical treatment with huge stained-glass windows, choir stalls and Gothic stencilling on the walls and roof timbers. In the same room, Pugin's elaborate mantel, exhibited at the Medieval Court of the Great Exhibition of 1851, shows the emerging trend of Celtic Revival, with the Irish inscription 'Cead Mille Failte', or 100,000 welcomes.

The sixth Duke also spent large sums on extravagant renovation work at Chatsworth House and when the seventh Duke succeeded in 1858, he found the family estates in a condition of extreme splendour but severe indebtedness. The Dungarvan and Youghal parts of the Lismore estate were sold between 1859 and 1862, but in 1876, the seventh Duke still remained one of the largest landowners in the United Kingdom. He held nearly 200,000 acres, of which 60,000 were in Counties Waterford and Cork. The majority of the Waterford and Cork lands were sold after the 1903 Land Purchase Act and today Lismore Castle remains the only substantial property of the Dukes of Devonshire in Ireland.

The castle became the home of the younger son of the ninth Duke, Lord Charles Cavendish, who married Adele Astaire, the sister and former dancing partner of Fred Astaire. After the death of her husband, Adele returned to America but continued to visit Lismore each summer, during which time Fred Astaire was a frequent visitor.

The twelfth Duke, who succeeded to the title in 2004, continues to live primarily on the family's Chatsworth estate. His son and heir, Lord Burlington, maintains an apartment in the castle and in 2005 converted the west range into a contemporary art gallery, known as Lismore Castle Arts. Today, the superb castle gardens and arts centre are open to the public daily from April to September. The remainder of the castle is not open to the public, but is available for private rental where guests can enjoy all its splendour and privacy, whilst being looked after by the Duke's own personal staff. (www.lismorecastle.com and lismorecastlegardens.com)

Lough Cutra Castle

County Galway

IN 1798, COLONEL CHARLES VEREKER received the thanks of Parliament and a royal proclamation following his defeat of the French force that attempted an invasion at Killala Bay, between Counties Mayo and Sligo. The defeated French General Humbert said of him: 'I met many generals in Ireland, but the only soldier among them was Colonel Vereker.' The colonel was wounded in the battle and when offered a peerage in return for voting in favour of the Act of Union, of which he was a bitter opponent, stated, 'I have defended my country with my blood, and there is nothing in the gift of the Crown that would tempt me to betray her by my vote.'

In 1810, the colonel's uncle, John Prendergast Smyth, Viscount Gort, gave him the Lough Cutra estate, which amounted to 12,000 acres. At this time the estate was often referred to as Lough Cooter. There was no mansion house on the estate but his uncle had planned for an Italianate villa at a spot called Situation Hill on the shoreline of the lough, and had begun planting trees and forest to enhance the location. The colonel would inherit his uncle's title, and also presumed he would get the family fortune, so proposed building a large Gothic mansion, favouring a position on the opposite side of the lough to his uncle. The story goes that on a visit to the Isle of Wight, accompanied by the architect John Nash and the Prince Regent, the colonel saw Nash's own property, East Cowes Castle, on which he exclaimed, 'How I wish I could transport this Castle to the banks of Lough Cooter.' Nash replied, 'Give me fifty-thousand pounds and I will do it for you.'

Nash was subsequently employed to design the colonel's new castle, but the eventual cost was in fact closer to £80,000, around €6 million in today's money. Nash is well remembered for his work as George IV's protégé on Brighton Pavilion, Buckingham Palace and Regent's Park. His own taste was for the classical. 'I hate this Gothic style,' he was heard to complain. 'One window costs more trouble to design than two houses ought to do.' Nash did visit Ireland but the work at Lough Cutra was supervised by two brothers, James and George Richard Pain, who had been apprentices to Nash in England. Nash has often been accused of poor workmanship, and on occasion he substituted wooden battlements for stone as an economy, but owing to the knowledge and vigilance of the Pains, Lough Cutra was superbly built.

Massive ground works were necessary, building up a terrace from the side of the lough and blasting out solid rock to considerable depth. Nash's drawings of the front elevation of the castle survive, signed by him and dated October 1811. The work was still ongoing in 1817, when the *Limerick Gazette* reported that James Pain 'was surveying some part of the beautiful building now going forward at Lough Cooter Castle, County Galway, the intended mansion of Lord Viscount Gort, when the scaffolding on which he stood gave way, and he was precipitated from an eminence of four storeys high. His side first reached the ground, with the head inclining downwards – the collar bone has been broken, the brain has

View of castle from north-west.

(Clockwise from top): The Gough Room (Library); the Saloon; the Great Hall.

received a severe concussion, and several bruises on different parts of the body.' James made a full recovery, living until 1877 and becoming, along with his brother George, among the most respected architects of their time.

Nash's design was quite simple in plan and fairly modest in scale, consisting of just one round, one square and two octagonal towers, linked by a low two-storey battlemented range. It exuded a military robustness whilst relying on the lakeside setting for its picturesque charm. The interior comprises a long, plaster vaulted hall, ending in a round tower in which rises a circular staircase. Off the hall, a series of reception rooms overlook the lake and on the second floor a top-lighted corridor leads to various bedrooms. Much of the gardens, including the long approaches to the castle, are the work of garden designer John Sutherland, whose style is said to reflect that of Lancelot 'Capability' Brown.

Colonel Vereker's uncle died in 1817 and he succeeded to his title, becoming the second Viscount Gort. When it came to inheriting the family fortune, however, the Colonel was shocked to discover that his uncle, a somewhat extravagant bachelor, had left debts amounting to £60,000. He had himself incurred heavy liabilities in the construction

Dining room.

One of the many fine castle bedrooms.

of his beautiful castle and was now in considerable financial trouble. As a result, he was rather impoverished and following his death in 1842 so too was his son and heir, John Prendergast Vereker, third Viscount Gort. The third Viscount helped his tenants as best as he could during the years of the Great Famine, by not collecting rents and providing work on the estate. Unfortunately, this worsened his financial position and in 1851 Lough Cutra was offered for sale by order of the Encumbered Estates Court. The estate was divided into parcels of land with the castle purchased by James Caulfield, in trust for Mrs Ball, Superior of the Loreto Convent, Rathfarnham, County Dublin, for £17,000. Lord Gort moved to England, where through marriage, he came to own Nash's East Cowes Castle, the inspiration for his own former property.

The Sisters of Loreto found the castle unsuitable for their needs and three years later sold it on to Field Marshal Viscount Gough. Lord Gough was a military man who had begun his career with the Limerick Militia in 1793. He distinguished himself in numerous battles and conflicts across Africa, China, India, and the East and West Indies, being promoted through the ranks of captain, lieutenant colonel, major general, general and field marshal. He made considerable extensions to Lough Cutra Castle, adding a clock tower wing, and employed John Gregory Crace to redecorate the interior, adding Union Flags, war emblems and Latin mottos. The original printing blocks for the wallpaper were retained, enabling the paper to be reprinted and restored in the twentieth century.

In the late 1890s, the third Viscount Gough employed the architect George Ashlin to add a further extension to the north-west of the castle, which was used to house his grandfather's collection of military trophies. This was demolished in the 1950s with the cut stone then used in the restoration of Bunratty Castle, County Clare (see p. 42).

The Land Acts of the early twentieth century forced the sale of much of the Lough Cutra estate and, with the loss of rental income, Lord Gough came under increasing financial pressure. In 1928, the family converted part of the stable buildings into a comfortable residence. The castle was closed up and they continued living in the converted stables in much reduced circumstances. During the Second World War the castle was used to billet troops and in 1952 the estate was placed on the market. The purchaser, Standish Vereker, the seventh Viscount Gort, was the great-grandson of the man who had sold it to the Loreto Sisters a century earlier.

Lord Gort gave Lough Cutra to his great-niece, the Hon. Elizabeth Sidney, who in 1966 married Sir Humphrey Wakefield. A year after purchasing Lough Cutra, Lord Gort also brought Bunratty Castle, County Clare. The Wakefields set about restoring Lough Cutra, saving it from a state of near-dereliction. Nash's original plans for the castle were used and much of Lord Gough's additions removed. Extensive restoration was carried out to the castle's interior, which had suffered through years of neglect. The Wakefields divorced in 1971, and again the castle was placed on the market. It was purchased by the present owner's family who made it their home and continued with its restoration. In 2003, the castle roof was replaced and in recent years extensive work has been completed bringing bedrooms and bathrooms up to modern standards.

Whilst not open to the public, Lough Cutra is available for private hire, as well as hosting a variety of events. In recent times Lough Cutra has had many high-profile visitors, including the Prince of Wales and the Duchess of Cornwall. (www.loughcutra.com)

Malahide Castle

County Dublin

The large drawing room.

R ICHARD TALBOT WAS GRANTED the lordship, lands and harbour of Malahide by King Henry II in 1184. For the next 800 years, except for a brief period in the 1650s, the property remained in the possession of the Talbots, making Malahide one of the oldest estates in Ireland to be continuously inhabited by the same family. They first built a motte-and-bailey castle about two kilometres south-east of the present castle, later relocating to build a stone castle in the early fifteenth century.

The first historical reference to the castle records it granted to the Talbots in a royal patent of 1486. The earliest part of the castle is a rectangular three-storey tower, which was later surrounded by various additions and extensions to create the present castle. This early tower contains the Great Hall, the only medieval hall in Ireland to keep its original form and remain in domestic use until recent times. It was in the Great Hall that fourteen members of the Talbot family and their cousins sat down to eat breakfast before riding off to join James II's army at the Battle of the Boyne. The Irish cavalry was involved in the heaviest fighting of the day and many were killed, including all fourteen of the Talbots and their kin.

Towards the end of the fifteenth century a square extension was added to the eastern side of the earlier tower, and between 1560 and 1640, the four-storey west wing was added, giving the house a U-shaped floor plan. The castle was surrounded by a strong bawn wall with turrets and gates, reflecting its main purpose, which at that time was keeping those inside safe from enemy attack.

At the end of the seventeenth century, as Ireland became a safer place and the threat of assault diminished, the castle's defensive purpose became less important and attention instead changed to aesthetics and comfort. The castle's

The small drawing room.

Great Hall.

(L–r): Gentleman's dressing room in the north turret; castle bathroom.

outer fortifications were removed and it began to lose its castellated character. It was then often referred to as Malahide Court rather than Castle.

In the 1760s a fire gutted the west wing. It was rebuilt by Richard Talbot and his wife, Margaret O'Reilly, later created Baroness Talbot de Malahide, using probably the same architect or builder who designed a very similar wing at Margaret's family home, Ballinlough Castle in County Westmeath. The small tapestry-hung rooms that had previously occupied the wing were replaced with two magnificent drawing rooms. Externally, the rebuilt wing was given a Georgian Gothic character, with slender round corner towers at each end.

In the early decades of the nineteenth century, when the appetite for neo-Gothic architecture peaked, Malahide's castellated appearance was enhanced with the addition of the projecting entrance front on the south side of the castle, and later a round tower on the south-east corner, balancing the tower on the south-west corner. An external spiral staircase led to this new tower, allowing the tenants of the estate to come to pay their rents at the land agent's office inside, without passing through the more prestigious areas of the castle interior. The new entrance front also allowed for the creation of the ground-floor hall and the expansion and remodelling of the Oak Room, above the entrance at first-floor level.

The famous Oak Room derives its name from its many elaborate carved oak panels, all stained black, which cover the room from wall to ceiling. Tradition relates that the oak used came from the woods at nearby Oxmanstown, but on close inspection, it appears the panels actually come from many dismantled pieces of furniture. Some date from the sixteenth century and are of Flemish origin. The six carved panels showing biblical scenes opposite the windows were originally the doors of a large cabinet and are copies of frescos by Raphael in the Vatican.

The panel above the chimney piece, which depicts the Assumption and Coronation of the Virgin, was of particular significance to the Talbot family and formed part of a chapel or altar when the Talbots still adhered to the Catholic faith. Between 1653 and 1660, John Talbot was evicted from Malahide by Cromwell for his part in the rebellion of 1641 and banished to Connacht. Over these seven years, Cromwell's henchman Miles Corbet occupied the castle, and the Virgin was reported to have miraculously vanished from the panel, only returning when the Talbots regained the castle.

Corbet was a signatory to the death warrant of Charles I, and was duly captured and then hanged, drawn and quartered after the Restoration of Charles II. His ghost is supposedly one of Malahide's many spectres and still haunts the castle as punishment for destroying the nearby Malahide Abbey, the burial ground of the Talbots for many centuries. Malahide's most famous ghost, Puck, is a dwarfish bearded figure about a metre in height, who is said to haunt a staircase leading into the Great Hall. One authenticated account of his appearance related to a naval officer who had just been appointed to the coastguard station at Malahide and had received an invitation to dine at the castle. As he approached the castle entrance he was met by a strange taunting figure in a fantastic costume. Not liking to be made the subject of a joke, the officer threatened to knock this figure down unless he told him what he wanted. Not getting a reply he reached out his arms to grab the figure, but they passed straight through his body. Quite disturbed by this bizarre event, the officer ran up to the castle but was further rattled when he found the strange figure now looking down upon him from one of the antique portraits that hung on the dining-room wall.

James Talbot, the sixth Baron Malahide, introduced Jersey cattle to the estate farm in the early nineteenth century, selling their rich milk to Bewley's Café in Dublin. At the age of fifty he married Joyce Gunning Kerr, the eighteen-year-old daughter of a London theatre manager. The sixth Baron inherited an estate of about 3,000 acres and during his tenure sold off much of the land, leaving the castle surrounded by just 300 acres. He did not have any children and on his death in 1948, Malahide was inherited by his nephew, Milo Talbot.

Milo, an eccentric bachelor, had had a distinguished, if mysterious, career in the British Foreign Office. He worked for some years in the British Secret Service but was rumoured to have been an espionage agent working for the Soviet KGB. Milo and his sister, Rose, moved to Malahide when he retired from the Foreign Office in 1956, aged forty-five.

Milo was an enthusiastic gardener, botanist, and a plant specimen collector of international renown. He developed the magnificent 15 acres of gardens at Malahide, planting more than 4,500 different species that he collected from many parts of the southern hemisphere. Conscious that he did not have a closely related heir, he entered into negotiations with the Irish government with a view that Malahide Castle might become a state residence for the Taoiseach. Milo, however, died suddenly in 1973 at the age of sixty, before the deal was finalised. There were rumours that his death might not have been accidental. A post-mortem was not carried out and his sister, Rose, was seen promptly burning many papers relating to his former career.

Rose inherited Malahide Castle, as well as a 22,000-acre sheep farm, also called Malahide, in an area of north-east Tasmania called Fingal. The sheep farm had been begun in 1822 by a family member, the Hon. William Talbot. Faced with very substantial death duties, she was forced to sell the castle and move to Malahide in Tasmania, where she lived happily for more than thirty years, frequently returning to Ireland and England to visit friends. Rose died in 2009 at the age of ninety-three, severing the last living link between the Talbot family and their ancestral home.

In 1976, the castle's contents, heirlooms of the Talbots that had been collected over 800 years, were sold at a public auction that lasted three days. Dublin City Council brought the castle and 78 acres of surrounding parkland and gardens for £650,000. Much of the castle's contents had already been dispersed but fortunately the County Council, the National Gallery of Ireland and other sympathetic individuals purchased some of its furnishings, which were returned to the castle. Other pieces were collected from various sources. The 10-metre-long dining table that dominates the Great Hall came from Powerscourt House in County Wicklow, and the unusual oval mahogany wine coolers in the same room came from Doneraile House in County Cork.

Today, Fingal County Council owns and maintains Malahide Castle, whilst their partners, Shannon Heritage, operate its day-to-day running. The castle is open to the public daily, year round. (www.malahidecastleandgardens.ie)

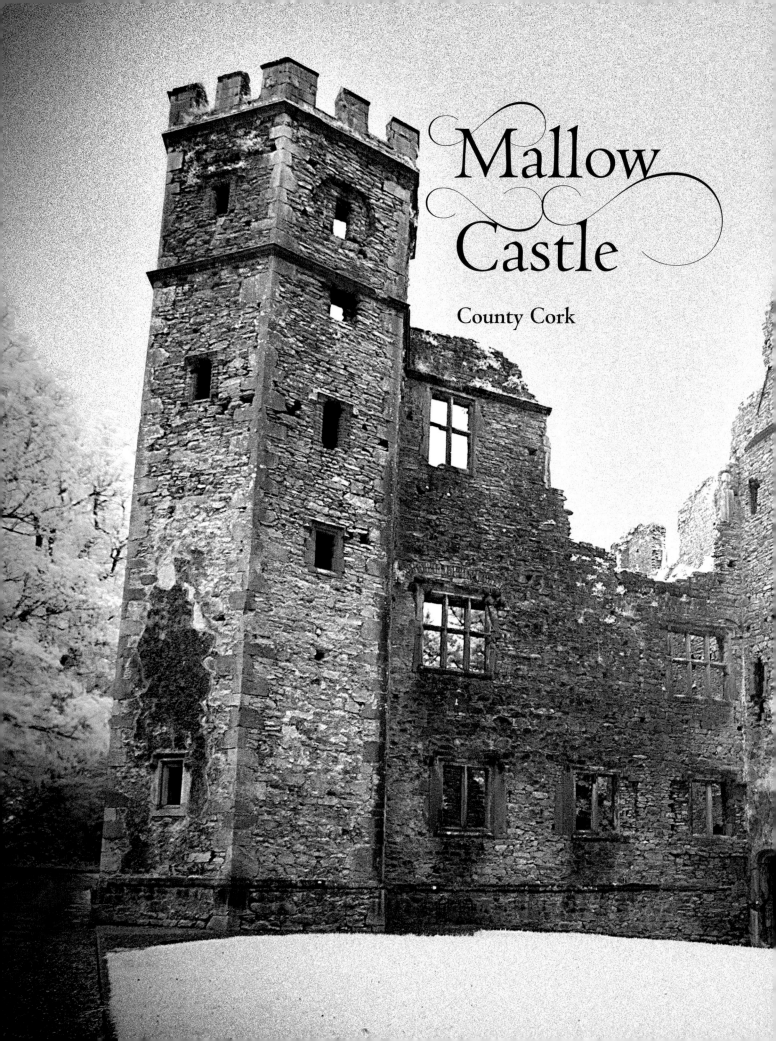

Mallow Castle

County Cork

Aerial view from south-west with mansion house in background.

THE FIRST STRONGHOLD AT MALLOW, probably a motte-and-bailey castle, was built by Prince John, later King John I, the youngest of King Henry II's five sons, who was Lord of Ireland in 1177. By 1282, the Desmond Geraldines had acquired the property and here they built a stone castle. In 1584, it was recorded as comprising a hall with a tower at the west end, contained within a bawn and two courtyards. The hall was two storeys high with a vault over the ground floor, a thatched roof, and measured about 8 metres by 18 metres. The tower was five storeys high with a vault over the third floor. This fortress was in the possession of the brother of the Earl of Desmond, Sir John, who played an active part in the Desmond Rebellion, and was captured, executed and his castle forfeited in 1584.

The castle and 6,000 acres were then granted by Queen Elizabeth I to Sir Thomas Norreys, Vice President of Munster, who succeeded as Lord President of Munster after the death of his brother, Sir John Norreys, in 1597. The Norreys brothers' grandfather, Sir Henry Norreys, had not fared well with King Henry VIII. He had been accused of sleeping with Queen Anne Boleyn just a few weeks after the birth of her daughter, the future Queen Elizabeth. Both he and Anne Boleyn were found guilty and executed. Queen Elizabeth always honoured Sir Henry Norreys' memory, believing that he died in a noble cause and in the justification of her mother's innocence, and so found great favour with the Norreys family.

Sir Thomas Norreys came to live at Mallow, where he found the castle had been badly damaged during the troubles of the Desmond rebellion. He demolished this earlier castle, and began building a large fortified house about 40 metres to the north-west. It is constructed of red sandstone with limestone dressings, and was originally plastered. Comprising a three-storey rectangular block, it has two octagonal four-storey corner turrets, one at the north-west corner, which contained a wooden spiral staircase, and one at the south-west corner. Two centrally placed wings project from the front and rear walls. All the floors were wooden and their positions can still be identified by the lines of joist sockets.

(L–r): View into castle interior; north interior wall.

Sir Thomas died in 1599, aged forty-three, after being wounded in an ambush at Kilteeley, County Limerick. His wife, Bridget, was left destitute and in poor health. In 1598, she had visited the astrologer Simon Forman, who wrote in his diary 'She hath a truckling in her flesh, like the stinging of nettles, and a rising of blood into her lungs, periplomania, much gravel in the veins, catarrh, fearfulness and trembling, she is often in great pain.' Forman notes that she was just twenty-four years old and her troubles were seemingly caused by a botched abortion. Bridget wrote to Sir Walter Raleigh asking for assistance, but died a year after her husband, in 1600.

Their four-year-old daughter, Elizabeth, who was Queen Elizabeth's namesake and godchild, inherited the Mallow property. The story goes that the Queen sent her godchild two white deer as a christening gift, and the herd of white deer at Mallow today is descended from this original pair. Elizabeth was married off to Major General Sir John Jephson at the tender age of just fourteen, and a year later she gave birth to a son, William.

In 1622, Mallow Castle is recorded by the commissioners who surveyed the area for the Plantation of Munster, as follows: 'There was built at Mallow by Sir Thomas Norreys, a goodly strong and sumptuous house, upon the ruins of the old castle, with a bawn to it about 120 foot square and 18 foot in height and many convenient houses of office.'

William Jephson inherited estates in England as well as in Mallow. He became a politician, sitting in the House of Commons from 1640 to 1648. In November 1641, he was in Ireland at the time of the outbreak of the rebellion in Munster. He raised a troop of horse guards at his own expense, and was commended for bravery by the Lord President, William St Leger. In 1642, Mallow Castle came under attack by the Catholic Confederacy. Arthur Bettesworth successfully defended it with a garrison of 200 men, one cannon and two light muskets. In 1645, the castle was again attacked and this time was taken by Lord Castlehaven and badly damaged.

William became a firm supporter of Oliver Cromwell, even suggesting that Cromwell take the title of King. He represented Cork in the First and Second Protectorate Parliaments of 1654 to 1658, and was then appointed envoy extraordinary to the King of Sweden. He died in 1658, recording in his will: 'I encourage my wife to live in Ireland which I hope God will incline her to do for her poor children's sake, I desire that she may live in my house at Mallow, which I give to her for life … if she will live there until my son and heir comes of age.'

William's descendants did indeed continue on at Mallow. In 1613, James I had granted a charter making the town a manor borough with the privilege of sending two Members to Parliament in Dublin. This charter was renewed in 1689 and so Mallow became treated as a pocket borough with the consequence that from 1692 until well into the nineteenth century every head of the Jephson family was also a Member of Parliament.

Less than a century after it had been built, Mallow Castle was destroyed by fire during the Williamite–Jacobite War. The Jephsons abandoned the castle, retreating to its stables and outbuildings, which were rebuilt as a comfortable home. Various changes were carried out to this house throughout the eighteenth century and in this time Mallow became fantastically famous for its social goings-on, becoming known as 'The Bath of Ireland'. The gentry visited from all over the country and their wild, rowdy behaviour was recorded in a 1740 song, 'The Rakes of Mallow':

> Beauing, belleing, dancing, drinking,
> Breaking windows, cursing, sinking,
> Ever raking, never thinking,
> Live the Rakes of Mallow;
> Spending faster than it comes,
> Beating waiters, bailiffs, duns,
> Bacchus' true begotten sons,
> Live the Rakes of Mallow.
> One time naught but claret drinking,
> Then like politicians, thinking
> To raise the 'sinking funds' when sinking.
> Live the Rakes of Mallow.
> When at home, with da-da dying,
> Still for mellow water crying;
> But, where there's good claret plying
> Live the Rakes of Mallow.

In 1837, Sir Denham Jephson, a direct descendant of the builder of the now-ruined castle, rebuilt and enlarged the converted stables, turning them into a fine mansion house. Sir Denham was MP for Mallow and in 1838 was created a baronet of Mallow in the County of Cork. The same year he assumed by royal licence the additional surname of Norreys.

View to mansion house.

View up in south-west corner tower.

Sir Denham acted largely as his own architect, though enlisted the help of Edward Blore, who is known for his work on Buckingham Palace, London. The mansion was given the appearance of an English manor house, with long, low and many-gabled ranges running either side of a three-storey battlemented tower. Sir Denham intended to add the entrance wing at the east end of the mansion and had the stonework cut and ready to use, but it sat in storage until 1954, when the house was further extended by his heir, Brigadier Maurice Denham Jephson.

Brigadier Jephson and his wife were killed in an Aer Lingus plane crash when Flight 712 went into the sea off Tuskar Rock, County Wexford, in 1968. The Mallow estate then passed to a distant cousin, Lieutenant Commander Maurice Jephson, who had taken part in the sinking of the German battleship *Bismarck* in May 1941. In 1982, the Lieutenant Commander sold the Mallow estate to the McGinn family of Washington DC, and in turn the McGinns sold it to Cork County Council in 2011.

In 1928, the old castle was made a National Monument and in 1933 its heavy growth of ivy was removed and the walls were repaired and stabilised. Today it is freely open to the public (although the manor house is not).

One curious story about Mallow Castle relates to Sir John Jephson, whose love of pleasure apparently far exceeded his income, resulting in many debts. One evening a strange gentleman asked for a private audience and when admitted to Jephson's study, laid down a heavy bag of gold, asking if he wished to be free of debt. Jephson jumped at this chance. The stranger then brought out a white rat, informing him that if he wanted comfort for the rest of his life, all he had to do was never eat anything without having the small creature on a small chair at his right-hand side. If he ever failed to do this, the consequences would be fatal. For many long years Jephson upheld this bizarre ritual, until at one banquet his guests showed such scorn and contempt that the rodent was removed from the dining table. After the guests had left, the strange gentlemen appeared again and taking up poor Jephson in his arms, smashed through a window and flew off with him. Jephson was never seen alive again and the window thereafter proved quite impossible to repair, despite many attempts to fix it. The white rat then often appeared before the head of the Jephson family, predicting their imminent demise.

Menlo Castle

County Galway

Menlo (Menlough) Castle was home to the Blake family from the beginning of the seventeenth century until it was destroyed in an accidental fire on 26 July 1910. The Blakes' origins in Ireland are thought to stem from the Welsh knight Sir Walter Caddell, who arrived on board Strongbow's ship during the 1169 Anglo-Norman invasion of Ireland. Historical documents refer to Walter's grandson as Richard Caddell 'Nigro' or 'Niger' on account of his dark skin. Within a generation or two 'Nigro' was anglicised to Blak (Black) and then Blake, and in 1346, his descendant, Walter Blake, is noted as burgess of Galway.

The Blakes became one of the fourteen Tribes of Galway, non-Gaelic, Catholic merchant families who dominated the commercial, political and social life of Galway in medieval times through to the late nineteenth century. In 1622, Valentine Blake, described as the richest man in Galway, was created Baronet Blake in the Baronetage of Ireland.

The first castle at Menlo beside the River Corrib was a tower house typical of the mid-sixteenth century. It was occupied by Thomas Coleman, a public notary of Galway town in 1561. Thomas's son Edmond sold the tower house to Sir Thomas Blake, the second Baronet, in the early years of the seventeenth century. Sir Thomas was MP for Galway Borough in 1634 and Mayor of Galway in 1637. Dying in 1642, he was succeeded by his eldest son, Sir Valentine Blake, third Baronet. Valentine followed in his father's political footsteps, becoming MP for County Galway in 1634, MP for Galway Borough in 1639, and Mayor of Galway in 1643.

Valentine fought against Cromwell's army during the 1651 Siege of Galway and after the surrender of the town to Sir Charles Coote, he was taken as a hostage. His death, a year later, was in sad circumstances. He was a high-spirited man and, after a quarrel with another gentleman, he determined that the matter would be best settled with a duel. Having mortally wounded his opponent he was about to leave the field when the dying man requested him to return and shake hands with him. This, however, was a trick and his adversary withdrew a concealed pistol and shot Valentine in the chest.

On Valentine's death, his extensive estates, which included Menlo and also property in Counties Clare, Galway and Mayo, as well as in Galway city, were confiscated by the Cromwellian government. It took the restoration of King Charles II, who was sympathetic to Catholics, to see the restoration of some of the Blake lands to Valentine's widow,

View of the castle from west.

View to castle interior through wall breach.

who was declared 'an innocent Papist'. Valentine's brother, Walter Blake, eventually recovered the Menlo property for his nephews.

The Blakes continued on at Menlo for the next two and a half centuries, expanding and extending the castle to suit their needs. By the start of the nineteenth century, the original tower house formed the north-east corner of an elaborate country mansion.

Menlo was the scene of much high living in the eighteenth and early nineteenth centuries. Sir John Blake ran up considerable debts with all his entertaining, and the story goes that he was made an MP to give him impunity from his creditors. After his election, his constituents arrived in a crowd at Menlo to find Sir John taking refuge from two debt collectors by hiding in a boat moored on River Corrib just downstream of the castle.

During the nineteenth century, Menlo was well known to Galway people for 'Maying at Menlo', when for several days the castle grounds were open to one and all. Steamboats ferried huge crowds from Woodquay in Galway city and celebrations were laid on for music, dancing and festivities. Numerous competitions were held for athletics, weight-throwing, tennis, swimming, rowing, yachting and tents and stalls sold all kinds of items like beer, porter and lemonade, fruits, sweets and other treats.

The castle came to a gloomy end on 26 July 1910. At 5.40 a.m. a groom named James Kirwan, who slept in the castle wing, was woken by the shouting of two female servants. On getting out of bed and opening his bedroom door, he was almost suffocated with smoke. Unable to proceed down the staircase, he threw his clothes out of his bedroom window and clambered, half naked, down the ivy growing up the outside of the castle. On reaching the ground, he found the two women had escaped the acrid smoke that filled the house and were now stuck on the roof over 10 metres from the ground. He begged them to keep still while he fetched help. He soon returned with two local men, named

Overgrown castle interior. The earliest part of the castle is the medieval wall at rear.

(L–r): Interior wall. Note the early fireplace at the bottom where the basement level is partly filled with debris; monument to Eleanor Blake, a little north-east of the castle.

EXPLORING IRELAND'S CASTLES

MENLOUGH CASTLE, GALWAY.

(L–r): Grave of Sir Valentine Blake, headstone deliberately placed over his feet; postcard of Menlo Castle (c. 1905).

Ward and Faherty, carrying a ladder but it proved to be too short to reach the women on the roof. The poor women were now screaming in agony as the red-hot roof slates burnt them. As a last resort the men placed piles of hay on the ground and then shouted at the women to jump. Delia Early jumped first and, landing on her head, was killed instantly by the fall. Annie Browne survived but landed on her hands and was badly injured. Kirwan now got on a horse and galloped to the police barracks in Galway to fetch help. District Inspector Mercer and a number of his men immediately set off for Menlo on bicycles and the fire brigade soon followed with about fifty men. Their attempt to douse the flames, however, was hopeless. By 7.00 a.m. the roof had fallen in and the castle was totally gutted. Its entire contents, including numerous paintings, tapestries, antique furniture and silver, the accumulation of three centuries' worth of the Blakes' treasured heirlooms, had all been destroyed.

At the time of the fire Sir Valentine and Lady Blake were in Dublin where Sir Valentine was undergoing an eye operation. The only member of the Blake family in the castle, their daughter, Miss Eleanor Blake, sadly perished in the flames.

Sir Valentine Blake died in 1912 and was buried in the graveyard about a kilometre north of the castle. A large police presence ensured the events seen at Valentine's father's funeral were not repeated: his father, Sir Thomas Blake, had been a devout Catholic since his youth and frequently attended Mass at St Nicholas' Church in Galway. Valentine, however, had his father buried as a Protestant, insisting he had a 'softening of the brain' that had impaired his judgment. The Menlo locals were greatly angered and a riot at the funeral had to be quelled by the parish priest. The locals were evidently still disgruntled and a headstone later erected on Valentine's own grave was deliberately placed over his feet.

In 1923, the Land Commission divided the Menlo estate amongst local farmers and the castle was left as an abandoned ruin. In 2000, Galway City Council issued a compulsory purchase order for the castle and there are hopes that the ruin will eventually be restored for public use.

Monea Castle

County Fermanagh

Monea Castle is the largest and best preserved of the plantation castles in Ulster. The Plantation of Ulster began in 1609. Following the Nine Years' War, the Flight of the Earls in 1607 saw Hugh O'Neill, Earl of Tyrone, Rory O'Donnell, Earl of Tyrconnell, and about ninety of their followers leave Ireland to seek Spanish help for a new rebellion. As a way to prevent further rebellion, their lands, comprising about half a million acres, were confiscated and used to plant, or colonise, Ulster with settlers loyal to the Crown. The principal new landowners were called undertakers, wealthy men from England and Scotland who undertook certain conditions in return for a 'proportion' of land between 1,000 and 3,000 profitable acres. In return, the undertaker was required to build a stone castle and bawn within three years and 'plant' twenty-four able men over the age of eighteen, of English or Scottish origin, for every 1,000 acres received.

Monea Castle was built by Reverend Malcolm Hamilton, a Scot, whose father, Sir Robert Hamilton, had received 1,500 acres in the plantation. Captain Nicholas Pynnar recorded a visit to the castle in his Survey of Ulster made in 1619–1620:

> Upon this proportion, there is a strong castle of lime and stone, being fifty-four feet long, and twenty feet broad; but hath no bawne unto it, nor any other defence for the succouring or relieving his tenants. I find planted and estated upon this land of British birth and descent: three freeholders, one having 384 acres, one having 120 acres, one having 60 acres, eleven lessees, three having 180 acres jointly, three having 120 acres a piece, two having 40 acres a piece, one having 20 acres. Of all these fourteen tenants, there are seven of them have taken the Oath of Supremacy, and these have diverse under-tenants under them, all which are able to make seventy-seven men with reasonable arms. There is good store of tillage, and not an Irish family on all the land.

Interior view from east.

View of castle from west.

Nature taking root in the castle interior.

View upwards in corner tower.

The bawn wall had been added by 1622 and originally rose to a height of about 4 metres with flanking towers on the opposing corners to the tower. Today, the remains of the tower at the north-west has *boulins* (pigeon holes) in the interior walls, indicating that it was later used as a dovecote.

Monea Castle originally stood three storeys high with tall attics and a slated roof. At the west end, a pair of massive semi-cylindrical towers provided a defensive position over the castle entrance. Distinctly Scottish in style, the towers feature crow-step gables and corbelled courses of carved stone. Similar towers can be seen still intact at Claypotts Castle near Dundee in Scotland. Inside the castle, the gloomy vaulted basement was lit only by musket loops and contained the kitchens and wine cellar. The principal rooms were on the first floor and were illuminated by large windows with seats in the embrasures. On the second floor were bedchambers and latrines with a chute that emptied outside the east wall.

Reverend Hamilton was appointed Rector of Devinish in 1622 and had a chapel at Monea that was more convenient and larger than Devinish Church, which was near the ancient priory on Devinish Island in Lough Erne. Hamilton's chapel was later rebuilt as the present Church of Ireland church at Monea, to where the east window of Devinish Church was relocated. Reverend Hamilton was advanced to the archbishopric of Cashel in 1623 and, after dying of fever in 1629, was buried in Cashel Cathedral, County Tipperary. His eldest son, Archibald, succeeded to the archbishopric of Cashel. His fourth son, also called Malcom, inherited the Fermanagh estate.

In 1641, Monea Castle was attacked by an army of men under the rebel leader Rory Maguire. According to an eyewitness, eight people inside the castle were killed but Maguire's men failed to capture the castle. It remained home to the Hamilton family and in 1688 was occupied by Gustavus Hamilton, Governor of Enniskillen. The castle was finally abandoned after a fire in about 1750. Its spiral stairs were deliberately broken at the start of the nineteenth century by Owen Keenan to stop his family of young boys enjoying their dangerous pastime of climbing to the most perilous parts of the crumbling walls. Shortly after, a woman named Bell McCabe, thought to be a witch, was forcibly evicted from a vault beneath one of the towers.

Monea Castle was taken into state care in 1954 and is freely open to the public.

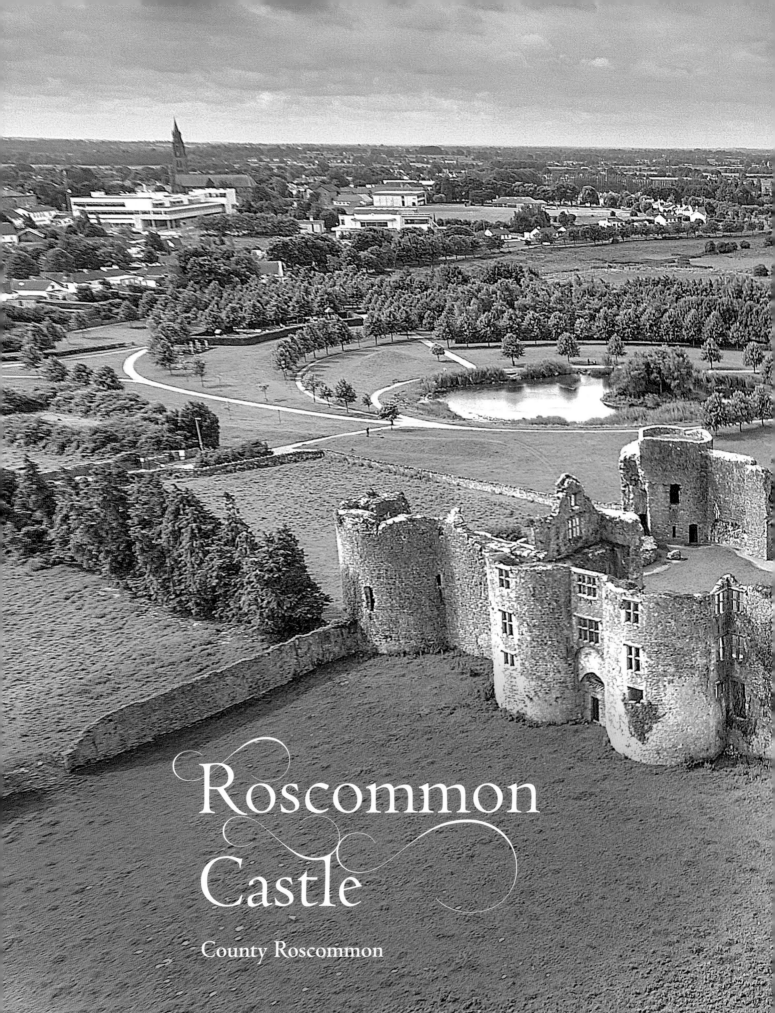

Roscommon Castle

County Roscommon

View to remains of fortified house in north of castle courtyard.

A HUNDRED YEARS AFTER THE ANGLO-NORMAN invasion and the formal submission of many of the Irish chiefs to Henry II as Lord of Ireland, control by the English Crown could still only be enforced in a small part of the island. In an attempt to gain effective rule over the troublesome outlying areas, the Crown embarked on a programme of castle-building.

The construction of Roscommon Castle began in 1269, under the instruction of Robert de Ufford, Chief Governor in Ireland for Henry III. Hugh O'Connor, King of Connacht, was an ardent opposer of the English, and burnt the unfinished castle in 1270, 1271 and 1272. After Hugh's death in 1274, the pace of construction increased dramatically, but the Irish forces attacked again in 1277 and demolished everything that had been built. This incited the English to build a stronger and more impregnable fortress, which progressed from 1280 to 1285. The castle faced constant attack and by 1304 its two portcullises and three drawbridges all needed major repairs.

Roscommon Castle is a keep-less castle, with a nearly rectangular courtyard measuring about 53 metres by 38 metres. The D-shaped towers at each corner all had three storeys, except the one at the north-west which had only two. The main gatehouse was on the eastern side and consisted of two D-shaped towers forming a rectangular block with a 3-metre-wide entrance passage between the towers. Only the curving walls of the towers survive above the foundations, where they were later incorporated into a fortified house. There is a smaller western gatehouse, through which the visitor enters the castle today, with a vaulted entrance passage with murder hole and drawbridge.

Roscommon Castle became the centre of Anglo-Norman power over a wide area of Ireland and was one of the primary royal castles in Ireland until the middle of the fourteenth century. It was attacked repeatedly and eventually taken by the O'Connors, who then held the castle until it was surrendered to the Dublin government in 1569.

In 1577, it was granted, along with 17,000 acres, to the English soldier and administrator Sir Nicholas Malby. Malby constructed a fortified house in the northern half of the courtyard. He also removed some of the 2.5-metre-deep outer moat, which once surrounded the castle, and built an extensive walled garden and a fishpond. A grand tree-lined avenue was also added, which led from the castle to Roscommon town.

View of original castle entrance from east (visitors now enter from the west).

(L–r) View of a castle stairway; interior view of south-western tower; view of north-east corner tower.

The castle was attacked by Red Hugh O'Donnell in 1596 and again in 1599. It was also a scene of strife during the Confederate Wars of the 1640s and was surrendered to a Cromwellian force in 1652. After the Williamite Wars of the 1690s the castle fell out of use.

Today, the castle is in the care of the OPW and is freely open to the public.

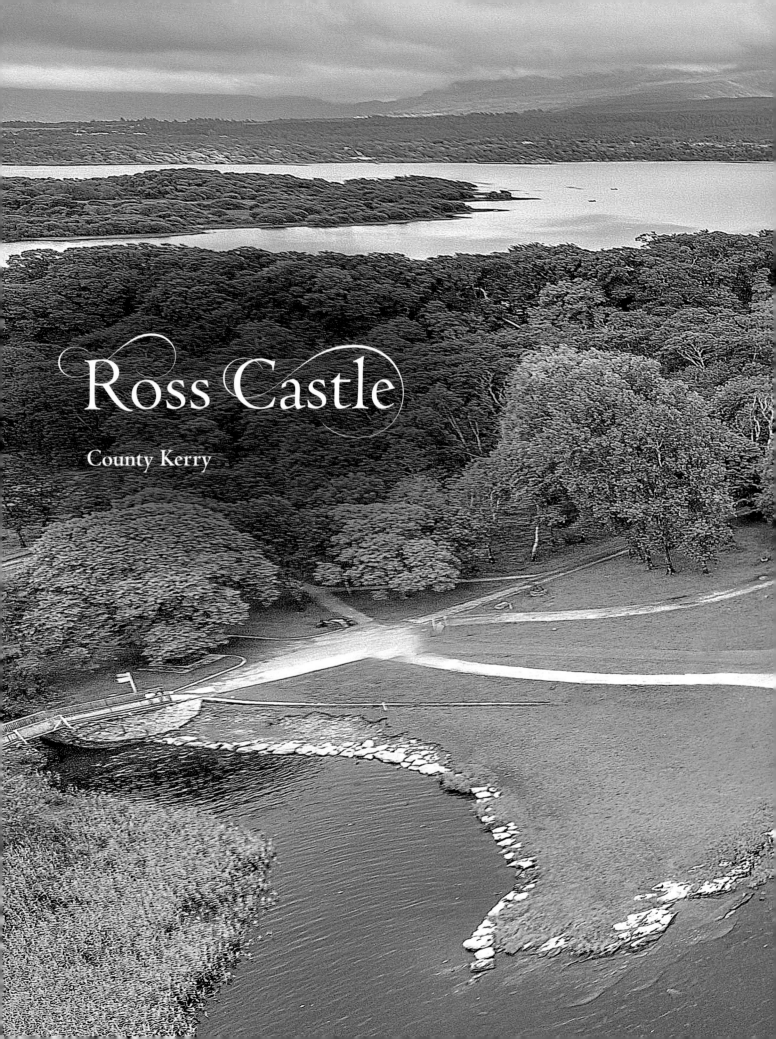

Ross Castle

County Kerry

View of castle from north.

Ross Castle was built in the late fifteenth century by one of the O'Donoghue Mór chieftains, hereditary rulers of the area and descendants of the ancient kings of Munster. The castle is built on a limestone outcrop on Ross Island, a peninsula separated from the mainland by a narrow channel. The original structure comprised a tower house surrounded by a fortified bawn, with circular flanking towers. Much of the bawn wall and two of the flanking towers were removed in the eighteenth century when a mansion house was added to the south of the tower and the quay was built along the lakeshore.

The tower house is typical of the strongholds of Irish chieftains built during the Middle Ages. Above ground level there are a further three storeys and the roof, with stone vaults above the ground floor and between the second and third storeys. The entrance, on the north side, was originally protected with an iron gate and leads to a small anteroom from where a murder hole in the ceiling would allow the castle garrison to pour burning oil or throw spears down on any enemy force. From the anteroom, a door to the main ground-floor chamber was constructed of two heavy layers of Irish oak. The layers of the door were bound by iron spikes, which originally protruded about 10 centimetres to the outer side, designed to impale an enemy attempting to force the door. A spiral staircase on the north-east corner of the tower runs in the typical clockwise direction, meaning a right-handed attacker climbing the stairs would have difficulty swinging a sword because of the stairs' central pillar. The stairs are also deliberately of uneven height, making them troublesome for those unfamiliar with their use.

The ground floor of the castle was used for storage and as an area of refuge during times of strife for those living around the castle. The next three floors each contain one large chamber and other ancillary rooms. The second floor is currently laid out as a bedchamber and has a fine reconstructed vaulted ceiling. The original ceiling collapsed though some areas remained in place. These were copied, allowing the entire ceiling to be rebuilt using the original medieval building techniques, where the stone was laid over a woven wickerwork frame and then finished with a plaster made of lime, sand and coarse animal hair. The top floor, the Great Hall, has two large six-light windows and a fine fireplace.

The original castle entrance. Today, visitors enter from a door in the east wall.

The Great Hall on the top floor. The roof is a modern reconstruction using original building methods.

First-floor chamber.

EXPLORING IRELAND'S CASTLES

The roof and minstrels' gallery are modern reconstructions, pegged together, as in the original, with oak dowels and do not contain any nails or screws. The spiral stairs continue upwards to the rooftop where a battlemented wall walk and bartizans provided safe points from where the castle garrison could fire arrows or drop rocks, burning oil or spears on any unwelcome visitors. The projecting stone brackets at roof level over the entrance door are a rare feature for an Irish castle. These would have supported an oak door which soldiers would push open to drop missiles on the enemy below, then retreat, allowing the door to close, blocking any return fire of arrows from the enemy.

Ross Castle remained the stronghold of the O'Donoghue Mór chieftains for about a 100 years. The sixteenth century saw the increasing strength of English rule in Ireland and the passing in 1542 of Crown of Ireland Act by the Irish Parliament, which made Henry VIII of England also King of Ireland. In 1562, the Earl of Desmond had had enough of English interference in his Munster territory and he rose up in rebellion. Fighting continued sporadically until 1583, when the Earl was finally hunted down and killed in the Slieve Mish Mountains in Kerry. His head was sent to Queen Elizabeth I and his body triumphantly displayed on the walls of Cork. Rory O'Donoghue Mór, an ally of the Earl of Desmond, was also killed and his support of the rebellion meant his entire lands were declared forfeit and seized by the Crown.

Ross Castle and the Killarney estate were acquired by Donal MacCarthy Mór and in turn mortgaged to Sir Valentine Browne, who had come to Ireland to survey the lands of Munster and facilitate its plantation. In about 1588, the collapse of the MacCarthy fortunes saw the Killarney estate come directly into Sir Valentine's hands. The Browne family soon married into the leading families of the old Gaelic aristocracy, eventually extending their land holdings to over 137,000 acres.

In 1652, the young Sir Valentine Browne, a descendant of the earlier Valentine, was in the care of his uncle, Cormac MacCarthy Mór, Lord Muskerry, who commanded the Munster forces of the Confederate Catholics. After losing at the Battle of Knockiclashy, Lord Muskerry retreated to Ross Castle with a force of about 1,500 men, hotly pursued by General Ludlow, who was in command of the Parliamentary forces, which comprised about 1,500 men on foot and a further 700 on horse.

Not seeing any way to capture the castle, Ludlow took account of a legend that foretold the castle would fall to a warship that approached from the lake. He arranged for a number of ships to be prepared by carpenters in Kinsale such that they could be transported overland and quickly assembled at Ross. The boats arrived on 18 June 1652 and were assembled and launched on the lake. Four days later Lord Muskerry signed his surrender.

Sir Valentine Browne managed to avoid forfeiting the castle as he was then just twelve years old. In later years he added a large mansion house to the south side of the castle. He remained loyal to King James II and was rewarded with the title of Viscount Kenmare, but forfeited the estate in 1690, fleeing to France in exile with James after the Williamite victory. Ross Castle was then used as a military barracks, accommodating a governor and two companies of infantry.

The third Viscount Kenmare managed to recover his estates and in 1726 built Kenmare House in Killarney town. The garrison left Ross Castle in 1825 and the then Lord Kenmare had the roof of the mansion removed and its large windows replaced with narrow loops, to reflect the style of the castle. By this time Killarney had been firmly established as a tourist destination, which became even more popular and prosperous after the visit of Queen Victoria and Prince Albert in August 1861.

Ross Castle was left to fall into ruin, becoming a well-photographed, romantic, ivy-covered ruin. In 1956, following the death of the seventh and last Earl of Kenmare, most of the Killarney estate, including Ross Castle, was sold to an American syndicate, which in turn sold the property two years later to John McShain. In 1970, Ross Castle was taken into state care and following extensive structural repair and restoration, which saw the roof replaced using medieval carpentry techniques as well as massive rebuilding of walls and ceilings, the castle was opened to the public in 1990.

Today Ross Castle is managed by the OPW and open to the public daily from March to November.

Scrabo Tower

County Down

SCRABO HILL, a long extinct volcano, derives its name from the Irish '*scrath bó*', meaning 'cow pasture'. According to the ballad 'The Fairy King's Courtship', the palace of a fairy king, Macananty, was under a great cairn on the hill's summit.

In 1857, the tower was erected on the top of Scrabo Hill as a monument dedicated to Charles William Vane-Stewart, the third Marquess of Londonderry. 'Fighting Charlie', as he was known, inherited the nearby family seat of Mount Stewart and succeeded to the title Marquess of Londonderry after his half-brother Robert Stewart, the second Marquess, better known as Viscount Castlereagh, took his own life in 1822.

Fighting Charlie had a distinguished and colourful career, rising through the ranks of the Fifth Royal Irish Dragoons and fighting in more than twenty-five famous battles. He was Adjutant General to the Duke of Wellington, received numerous foreign honours and honorary degrees from both Oxford and Cambridge, before being elected to the Irish House of Commons, and after the Act of Union, representing Londonderry in the British House of Commons. He was later admitted to the Privy Council, appointed a Lord of the Bedchamber to the King, as well as being made Ambassador to Vienna.

Coloured lithograph, from *The Illustrated London News*, 1857.

Despite these illustrious positions, he had a reputation for loutish behaviour and drunkenness. In Ireland he was seen as an absentee landlord who spent nearly all his time in London. By the 1840s he was one of the ten richest men in the country, but was criticised for his meanness when, during the Great Famine, he and his wife gave just £30 to the local relief committee but spent £15,000 renovating their Irish home, Mount Stewart. He may have been judged unfairly as the renovation works would have provided much local employment in a time of extreme hardship.

After his death in 1854, a meeting was held at Newtownards Rectory to discuss how the Marquess should be commemorated. A second meeting, held in the Imperial Hotel in Belfast in 1855, resolved that a monument should be constructed on Scrabo Hill and a competition would be held for the best design. The cost of the monument was not to exceed £2,000 and two prizes were offered, £20 for the best design and £15 for second place.

The competition received four entries. In first place was an obelisk by W. J. Barre of Newry, in second place a tower by J. Boyd of Belfast, in third a tower by Daniel Hanus, and in fourth a tower by Sir Charles Lanyon. Tenders were placed for the construction of all four monuments and when the cost of construction for the first three designs all came in at more than £2,000, Lanyon was declared the winner.

The ironic outcome was, however, that Lanyon's design ultimately proved too expensive and his tower had to be reduced in height, the buttress walls omitted, and the tower interior left incomplete. Even with these changes, the construction cost came in at over £3,000.

Scrabo Tower, County Down.

View of tower from north.

202

Mount Stewart, the Irish home of the Marquess of Londonderry.

Scrabo Tower stands 41 metres high and is built at a height of 165 metres above sea level, so it is visible from miles around. Its walls are over a metre thick and are made of stone quarried from the surrounding hill. The walls are constructed of dark dolerite rock, from the summit, while the window dressings, roof, stairs and quoins are constructed of local sandstone.

An inscribed panel above the doorway on the north side reads:

> Erected in memory of Charles William Vane
> 3rd Marquess of Londonderry KG and C by his tenantry and friends
> Fame belongs to history, remembrance to us 1857

The only family to occupy the tower were the McKays. William McKay was the quarry foreman and lived in the tower with his wife and eight children from the 1860s. Elizabeth, Jean and Agnes, William McKay's grandchildren, gave back the tower's keys to the Londonderry estate in 1966. The three sisters, all of whom were born in the tower, had run a tearoom which specialised in Irish country teas using goat's milk.

The tower was handed over to the Department of the Environment (NI) which undertook a restoration programme, repointing and replacing some of the stonework that had been damaged by rainwater penetration and lightning strikes. Following this, the tower was opened to the public in 1983. It now houses an exhibition on the Country Park and surrounding countryside. Visitors can climb the 122 steps to the rooftop viewing platform, from where the Isle of Man and the Scottish coast can be seen on clear days.

Trim Castle

County Meath

View of castle from north-west.

I N 1172, Hugh de Lacy, Lord of Meath, built a fortress on this site, comprising a ringwork castle, where an earthwork fortification was enclosed by a defensive ditch about 2 metres deep and 50 metres in diameter. He left it in the hands of Hugh Tyrrell, who a year later set fire to the structure and fled when facing attack by Roderick O'Connor, King of Connacht. De Lacy later married Roderick's daughter and started to rebuild the fortification in stone. It was completed by his son, Walter, and became the largest Anglo-Norman fortress in Ireland.

The massive central keep, with walls nearly 4 metres thick and reaching a height of 21 metres, is square in plan, with smaller square towers projecting from each of its sides. Three of these smaller towers survive and their purpose is obscure. Their walls are much thinner than those of the central tower and the additional angles increase their vulnerability rather than adding any defensive purpose. They may have been used to increase the number of chambers within the castle, or used only for aesthetics.

The main part of the keep is divided by a cross wall to the height of the first storey and had three storeys in total. The projecting towers have a fourth storey and there was a chapel on the second floor of the eastern tower. There is a clear break in the masonry about halfway up the walls, and a close examination reveals at least three main phases of construction as well as much repair and alteration. Analysis of tree rings from timbers recovered from the walls indicated that the three phases of construction took place around 1175, the 1190s and in the first years of the thirteenth century.

The outer curtain wall, two thirds of which still survives, was built on ground cut down to the bedrock, making it almost impossible to undermine. It was originally surrounded by a moat. The wall averages about 8 metres in height, nearly 2 metres in thickness and originally had a circuit of about 450 metres. It contains two levels of arrow loops and is studded with towers and two main gatehouses. The west gate facing the town, known as Trim Gate, is the earlier gateway and still serves as the castle's main entrance. It was protected by a drawbridge and a portcullis, the slots of

Outside the castle walls, view to barbican tower.

which survive inside the doorway. The outer face of the portcullis was protected from above by a murder hole, from where the guards could drop rocks or burning oil on any unwelcome visitor.

The Dublin Gate, on the south side, is a rare example with an external barbican tower. It comprises a round tower built into the curtain wall, with a narrow passageway spanning the moat, leading to the rectangular barbican on the exterior of the castle. The word 'barbican' comes from the Latin *barbecana*, meaning the outer fortification of a castle. Its main purpose was to confine people entering the castle into a narrow passage that was crossed by a drawbridge. A portcullis could be dropped at either end of the passage and murder holes above allowed arrows or missiles to be fired down on an enemy. The future Henry V lived in this gatehouse for a time, as a boy, around 1399.

Trim Castle changed hands a number of times before passing to the Geneville family when Walter de Lacy's granddaughter Matilda married Geoffrey de Geneville, and to the Mortimer family when Joanna de Geneville married Roger Mortimer.

In 1465, a parliament held at Trim gave permission for the beheading of anybody found guilty of theft and any head so cut off was to be placed on a spear in front of the castle. The beheader and those who helped him could then claim a payment from the landowner of where the robbery had taken place. About the same time the parliament decreed that coins would be minted at Trim Castle, predating the coinage of England by about 140 years. Two coins were struck in brass under the direction of Germyn Lynch, goldsmith of London, warden and master worker of the Trim mint. The Patrick's Farthing had a bishop's head on one side and a cross with roses and suns on the reverse. The half-farthing had a crown surrounded by roses on one side and a cross on the reverse.

In 1541, Henry VIII allocated £200 for substantial works on the castle dungeon, gates and walls. At this time there were twenty-two cottages in the town of Trim, and the occupants were obliged to provide labour service

Interior view of barbican tower.

Interior view of east side of keep.

towards the repair of the castle whenever called upon. For the remainder of the sixteenth century the castle fell increasingly into decline. It was refortified during the Irish Confederate Wars of the 1640s, and in 1647 Colonel Fenwicke occupied the fortress with a regiment of foot and some troops of horse.

Trim Castle remained in Royalists' hands until the fall of Drogheda in 1649, when that town was besieged and stormed by English Parliamentarian forces under the command of Oliver Cromwell. The garrison at Trim fled instead of obeying the Duke of Ormond's instructions to destroy the castle before letting it fall into the hands of Cromwell's army.

After the wars of the 1680s, the castle was granted to the Wellesley family who held it until Arthur Wellesley, Duke of Wellington, sold it to the Leslies. It later passed via the Encumbered Estates Court into the hands of the Dunsany Plunketts. They left the castle and surrounding lands unused and open, and from time to time allowed various uses, with part of the castle field rented for some years by Trim Town Council as a rubbish dump. In 1993, Lord Dunsany sold the land and buildings to the Irish state, retaining only river access and fishing rights.

The OPW began a major programme of exploratory works and conservation at a cost of over €6 million. This superb and exemplary work made the castle accessible to the public in 2000 and will preserve it for future generations. Today, the castle is open to the public at weekends during the winter months and daily from March to October.

The castle was used in the making of Mel Gibson's film *Braveheart* where it features in several scenes, including its massive gatehouse being portrayed as the entrance to the fortified English town of York, and London Square, which was recreated against the sides of the castle wall.

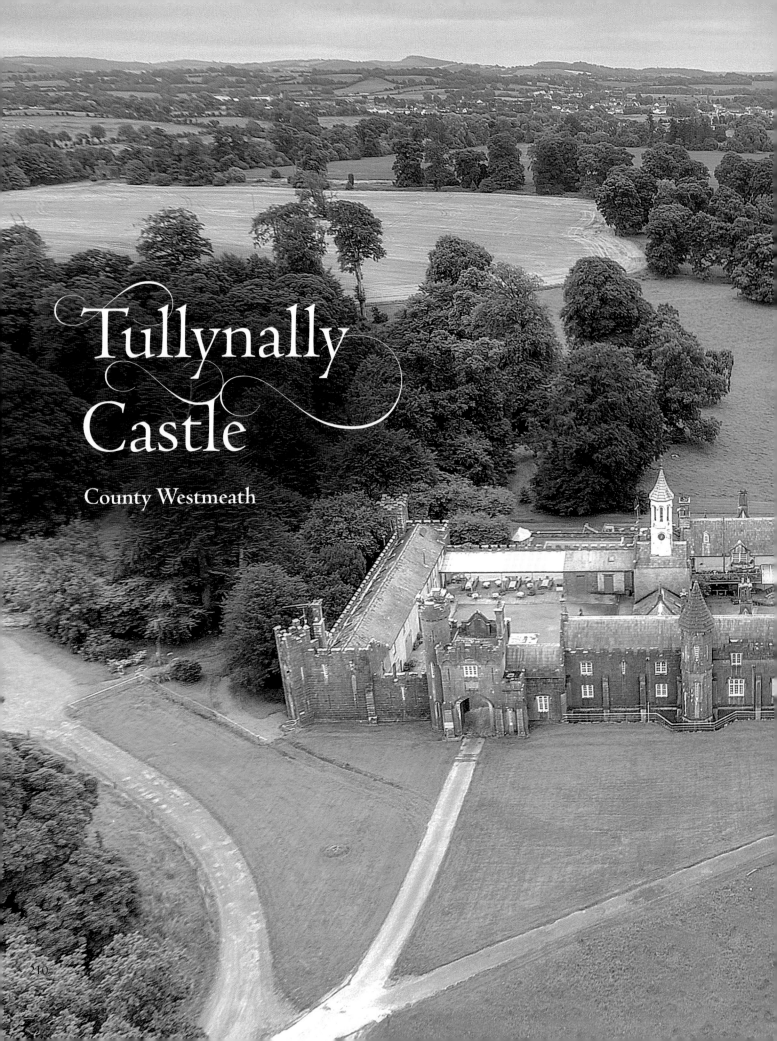

Tullynally Castle

County Westmeath

View east to entrance of castle stable yard.

THE PAKENHAMS, originally from Suffolk in England, first came to Ireland in 1576, when Sir Edward Pakenham was in the entourage of his cousin, Sir Henry Sidney, the Lord Deputy of Ireland. Nearly a century later, Sir Edward's grandson, Captain Henry Pakenham, was in the service of the Parliamentary Dragoons and in 1665 he was granted extensive lands in lieu of pay. He established himself at Tullynally, where he and his descendants built a comfortable mansion house, which they named Pakenham Hall.

A family diary of 1736 shows a small illustration of the house, and a description a year later records it as being an old two-storey building, measuring about 21 by 28 metres with an extensive, classically laid-out garden, typical of the early eighteenth century. In the gardens, water from a 100-metre-wide basin cascaded into another basin at the head of a vast canal, measuring over 40 metres wide and 350 metres long. The grassy banks of the canal were laid with walkways and planted with trees, with another stream taking the water a further mile to a terminating reservoir.

In 1739, Henry's grandson Thomas married a neighbouring heiress, Elizabeth Cuffe, the great niece of Ambrose Aungier, the second Earl of Longford. Elizabeth brought the town of Longford to the Pakenhams and also a considerable amount of land. Her inheritance paid for sizeable improvements to Pakenham Hall, including the addition of a third storey. The old formal gardens were also swept away as wild, romantic landscapes, in the style of the great English landscape gardener Lancelot 'Capability' Brown, became the fashion. Thomas was created Baron Longford in 1756, and after his death Elizabeth was created Countess of Longford in her own right. In 1780, their son, Edward, the second Baron Longford, employed Graham Myers, architect to Trinity College in Dublin, to carry out various improvements to the house. Ceiling heights on the ground floor were raised and windows were changed.

Edward died in 1792, and his son, Thomas, became the third Baron Longford and inherited Pakenham Hall. In 1794, on the death of his grandmother Elizabeth, Countess of Longford, Thomas also succeeded to the title Earl of Longford, becoming the second Earl. In 1801, he employed the eminent architect Francis Johnston to remodel Pakenham Hall, beginning its transformation from a plain Georgian mansion house into a neo-Gothic castle.

(Clockwise from top): The dining room, wallpaper designed by A. W. N. Pugin for the Houses of Parliament in London; the drawing room. The geometrical ceiling was designed by James Sheil and the four ebonised spoonback chairs on the left were described and sketched by Maria Edgeworth in 1811; the enormous vaulted entrance hall, forming the hub the castle.

Johnston's work included the addition of a battlemented parapet, and two round projecting turrets on the south-east and south-west corners. The alterations were made only a few years after the 1798 Rebellion, when several big houses had been burnt by rebels, and wealthy landlords were obvious targets. Bearing this in mind, Lord Longford specifically requested a portcullis entrance porch to be added to his house. Johnston's remodelling continued until 1806, by which time the house had become known as Pakenham Hall Castle.

The second Earl was good friends with the politician, writer and inventor Richard Lovell Edgeworth who, as part of the upgrades to Pakenham Hall, designed a central heating system, one of the earliest recorded in Britain and Ireland. His daughter, the prolific writer Maria Edgeworth, visited soon after the work was complete and wrote: 'Lord Longford has finished and furnished his castle which is now really a mansion fit for a nobleman of his fortune … the

The library with many books written by the Pakenham family displayed on the table. Portrait of Major General Sir Edward Pakenham above fireplace.

immense Hall so well warmed that the children play in it from morn till night.' Maria also added, 'Lord Longford has made such a comfortable nest he must certainly get some bird with pretty plumage and a sweet voice to fill it,' but it would actually take another decade for the second Earl to find a wife.

Many of Lord Longford's siblings had military connections. His sister Catherine, or Kitty, was married to the first Duke of Wellington; one brother, Lieutenant General Sir Hercules Robert Pakenham, served as aide-de-camp to William IV; another brother, Major General Sir Edward Pakenham, or Ned as he was affectionately known, was killed at the Battle of New Orleans in 1815. After his death, Ned's body was returned to Ireland in a cask of rum for purposes of preservation. He was known for his surly temper and it was said that he had returned home in better spirits than he left. Another story goes that the cask got mixed up with another and ended up in Barbados, where most of the contents were drunk before the body was discovered inside. This led to the invention of a drink, the 'Pakenham cocktail', a spicy mix of spirits and chilli pepper. Ned's posthumous portrait hangs over the polished limestone chimney piece in the castle library.

In 1817, the second Earl married Lady Georgina Lygon, an English heiress, and took enthusiastically to family life, having seven sons and three daughters. This seems to have prompted a second round of construction work on the castle and Johnston's former clerk, James Shiel, was employed as the architect. Shiel's remodelling included the addition of a three-sided bow on the garden front and the Gothicisation of many rooms, including the immense entrance hall.

EXPLORING IRELAND'S CASTLES

In the 1830s, the second Earl's wife, Lady Georgina, began creating the castle's wonderful gardens. Maria Edgeworth admired her work in one of her letters: 'I never saw in England and Ireland such beautiful gardens and shrubbery walks as she has made – In a place where there was only a swamp and an osiery, she has made the most beautiful American garden my eyes ever beheld – took advantage of a group of superb old chestnut trees, oak and ash for a background – trees that had never been noticed before in that terra incognita and now it is a fairy land.'

The second Earl sat in the British House of Lords as one of the twenty-eight original Irish Representative Peers. In 1821, he was created Baron Silchester, of Silchester in the County of Southampton, in the Peerage of the United Kingdom, which gave him and his descendants an automatic seat in the House of Lords.

The second Earl died in 1835 and his eldest son, Edward Michael Pakenham, became the third Earl. In 1839, when he was twenty-two years old, the trustees of the estate employed the eminent architect Sir Richard Morrison to extend the castle further. Morrison added two large castellated wings that linked the house with its stable block, almost doubling its size. One wing contained a private apartment with a billiard room on the ground floor; the other wing contained a vast kitchen, accommodation for a growing retinue of servants, and a state-of-the-art three-room laundry. The Longfords' laundry continued to be sent here by boat and train from their house in London, to be washed and then returned, until the start of the First World War.

Morrison was another advocate of the neo-Gothic and his additions, beautifully constructed of cut limestone, contain a fine array of battlements, turrets, crosses and arrow slits. The last addition to the castle was in 1860, when the fourth Earl, William Lygon Pakenham, employed the Dublin-based Scottish architect James Rawson Carroll to add a pinnacled tower at the north-east corner of the stable yard.

The fifth Earl, Thomas Pakenham, served as Lord Lieutenant of County Longford from 1887 until he was killed in action at Gallipoli in 1915. His eldest son, Edward Arthur Henry Pakenham, succeeded as the sixth Earl. He was a playwright and poet, chairman of the Gate Theatre in Dublin, and also sat as a member of Seanad Éireann between 1946 and 1948. When he died childless in 1961, his younger brother, Francis Aungier 'Frank' Pakenham, a prominent Labour politician and social activist, succeeded to the Longford title, becoming the seventh Earl, but the castle went to the seventh Earl's son, Thomas Pakenham.

Thomas studied classics and ancient history at Magdalen College, Oxford, and spent time in Ethiopia before becoming a journalist working for *The Observer*. In order to pay the sixth Earl's death duties, substantial properties in south County Dublin had to be sold, but Thomas managed to retain Pakenham Hall and its surrounding 1,500 acres. In 1964, he gave up his newspaper job and moved to Ireland where he renamed Pakenham Hall Tullynally Castle, reviving its ancient name. Tullynally derives from Gaelic, *Tulaigh an Eallaigh*, or the Hill of the Swan, for the hill overlooks Lough Derravaragh, the legendary lake of the Children of Lir who were turned into swans.

After transforming 1,000 acres of the estate into an intensive dairy operation, Thomas set about writing three large and successful history books, *The Year of Liberty*, *The Boer War* and *The Scramble for Africa*. His work transforming Tullynally's tired and overgrown gardens into the magnificent pleasure grounds that they are today led to a change of writing tack and so followed his very successful book, *Meetings with Remarkable Trees*. This book was made into a radio and television series, and was followed by a series of other books about trees. Thomas is a passionate gardener, arborist and is chairman of the Irish Tree Society. His wife, Valerie, is also a successful author and her books include *The Traveller's Companion to Dublin*, *Noonday Sun: Edwardians in the Tropics*, and *The Big House in Ireland*. Their daughter, Eliza, continued the tradition of writing and her work includes a family history of the Pakenhams, *Soldier, Sailor: an Intimate Portrait of an Irish Family*.

One of the most delightful rooms in the castle is the library, where oak bookcases line the walls from floor to ceiling, cocooning guests in the smell of leather and old paper. It contains more than 6,000 volumes spanning nearly four centuries, all carefully catalogued by Thomas Pakenham.

The Pakenham coat of arms on castle wall, with family motto '*Gloria Virtutis Umbra*' ('glory is the shadow of virtue').

Thomas says of his forebears: 'The Pakenhams were anti-show and anti-snob.' A very modest man, being the recipient of honorary doctorates from three Irish universities, he does not use the title doctor, or the Earl of Longford title that he inherited from his father.

The splendid Tullynally Castle gardens and tearooms are open to the public over weekends and bank holidays in April, May and September; and from Thursdays to Sundays and bank holidays in June, July and August. The castle interior is open on various occasions and to groups by previous arrangement. (www.tullynallycastle.ie)

Bibliography

Books

Adams, C. L., *Castles of Ireland* (London, 1904)

Agnew, A., *A History of the Hereditary Sheriffs of Galloway* (Edinburgh, 1864)

Barry, E., *Barrymore, records of the Barrys of County Cork* (Cork, 1902)

Bence-Jones, M., *A Guide to Irish Country Houses* (London, 1988)

Blake, M. J., *Blake Family Records 1600–1700* (London, 1902)

Blake, T. & Reilly, F., *Ancient Ireland* (Cork, 2013)

Blake-Forster, C., *The Irish Chieftains; or, A Struggle for the Crown* (Dublin, 1872)

Brewer, J. N., *The Beauties of Ireland* (London, 1826)

Browne, N., Castle Oliver and the Oliver Gascoignes (Limerick, 2008)

Burke, B., *A Genealogical and Heraldic Dictionary of the Landed Gentry of Great Britain and Ireland* (London, 1871)

Burke, B., *A Genealogical and Heraldic Dictionary of the Landed Gentry of Ireland* (London, 1912)

Burke, B., *A Genealogical History of the Dormant, Abeyant, Forfeited and Extinct Peerages of the British Empire* (London, 1883)

Carlyle , T., *Oliver Cromwell's Letters and Speeches* (New York, 1845)

Carrigan, W., *History and Antiquities of the Diocese of Ossory* (Dublin, 1905)

Charleville, C. M. D. B., *The Marlay letters, 1778–1820* (London, 1937)

Connellan, O., *The Annals of Ireland* (Dublin, 1846)

Cooke, T. L., *Early History of the Town of Birr or Parsonstown* (Dublin, 1875)

Coote, C., *General view of the agriculture and manufactures of the King's County* (Dublin, 1801)

Davis, T., *The Architecture of John Nash* (London, 1960)

De Breffny, B., *Castles of Ireland* (London, 1977)

Ellis, H., *Romances and Ballads of Ireland* (Dublin, 1850)

Fraser, J., *A Handbook for Travellers in Ireland* (Dublin, 1844)

Freeman-Attwood, M., *Leap Castle* (Norwich, 2001)

Gaul, L., *Johnstown Castle: A History* (Dublin, 2014)

Gribayedoff, V., *The French Invasion of Ireland in 98* (New York, 1890)

Griffiths, G., *Chronicles of the County of Wexford* (Enniscorthy, 1877)

Guinnes, D. & Ryan, W., *Irish Houses and Castles* (New York, 1971)

Howe Adams, J., *History of the Life of D. Hayes Agnew* (Philadelphia, 1892)

Howitt, W., *Ruined Abbeys and Castles of Great Britain and Ireland* (London, 1864)

Joyce, P. W., *Ancient Irish Music: Comprising One Hundred Airs Hitherto Unpublished* (Dublin, 1873)

Joyce, P. W., *Irish Local Names Explained* (Dublin, 1922)

Knight of Glin, *The Irish County House* (London, 2010)

Lacy, T., *Home Sketches, On Both Sides of the Channel* (London, 1852)

Leask, H. G., *Irish Castles and Castellated Houses* (Dundalk, 1941)

Leet, A., *A Directory to the Market Towns, Villages, Gentlemen's Seats, and Other Noted Places in Ireland* (Dublin, 1814)

Lewis, S., *A Topographical Dictionary of Ireland* (London, 1837)

Lynn, W. H., *Notes on the Ruins of Dunluce Castle, County of Antrim* (Belfast, 1905)

MacDonnell, R., *The Lost Houses of Ireland* (London, 2002)

McNeill, T., *Castles in Ireland* (London, 1997)

Morris, Rev. F. O., *Picturesque Views of Seats of the Noblemen and Gentlemen of Great Britain and Ireland* (London, 1880)

Nelson, P., *The Coinage of Ireland* (Liverpool, 1905)

O'Brien, G., *These My Friends and Forebears: The O'Briens of Dromoland* (Clare, 1991)

O'Byrne, R., *Romantic Irish Homes* (London, 2009)

O'Donovan, J., *The genealogies, tribes, and customs of Hy-Fiachrach, commonly called O'Dowda's Country* (Dublin, 1844)

O'Hanlon, J., *Irish Folk Lore: traditions and superstitions of the country* (London, 1870)

O'Reilly, S., *Irish Houses and Gardens* (London, 2008)

Pakenham, E., *Soldier, Sailor An Intimate Portrait of an Irish Family* (London, 2007)

Pakenham, V., *The Big House in Ireland* (1998, London)

Potterton, M., *Medieval Trim: History and Archaeology* (Dublin, 2005)

Pritchard, D., *Malahide Castle and Gardens* (Bunratty, 2012)

Rait, R. S., *The Story of an Irish Property* (Oxford, 1908)

Robertson, J. G., *Antiquities and Scenery of the County of Kilkenny* (Kilkenny, 1851)

Stafford, T., *Pacata Hibernia : or, A history of the wars in Ireland* (London, 1810)

Trimble, W. C., *History of Enniskillen* (Eniskillen, 1919)

Villiers-Tuthill, K., *History of Kylemore Castle & Abbey* (Galway, 2002)

White, J. G., *Historical and Topographical Notes etc. on Buttevant, Castletownroche, Doneraile, Mallow and places in their vicinity* (Cork, 1913)

Wilde, M. D., *Lough Corrib, Its Shores and Islands* (London, 1867)

Woods, J., *Annals of Westmeath Ancient and Modern* (Dublin, 1907)

Woulfe , Rev. P., *Irish Names and Surnames* (Dublin, 1922)

Wright, A. M., *A Guide to the Lakes of Killarney* (London, 1822)

Wright, J., *The King's County Directory* (Parsonstown, 1890)

Yeats, W. B., (ed.) *Irish Fairy Tales* (London, 1892)

Journals & Magazines

Analecta Hibernica

Archaeology Ireland

Archivium Hibernicum

History Ireland

Irish Arts Review

Journal of the Cork Historical & Archaeological Society

Journal of the Galway Archaeological and Historical Society

Kerry Archaeological Magazine

Proceedings and Transactions of the Kilkenny and South-East of Ireland Archaeological Society

Proceedings of the Royal Irish Academy

The Dublin Historical Record

The Dublin Penny Journal

The Illustrated Magazine of Art